SHEPHERD'S NOTES
Christian Classics

Shepherd's Notes Titles Available

SHEPHERD'S NOTES COMMENTARY SERIES

Old Testament

9-780-805-490-282 Genesis
9-780-805-490-565 Exodus
9-780-805-490-695 Leviticus, Numbers
9-780-805-490-275 Deuteronomy
9-780-805-490-589 Joshua, Judges
9-780-805-490-572 Ruth, Esther
9-780-805-490-633 1 & 2 Samuel
9-780-805-490-077 1 & 2 Kings
9-780-805-490-649 1 & 2 Chronicles
9-780-805-491-944 Ezra, Nehemiah
9-780-805-490-060 Job
9-780-805-493-399 Psalms 1-50

9-780-805-493-405 Psalms 51-100
9-780-805-493-412 Psalms 101-150
9-780-805-490-169 Proverbs
9-780-805-490-596 Ecclesiastes, Song of
Solomon
9-780-805-491-975 Isaiah
9-780-805-490-701 Jeremiah, Lamentations
9-780-805-490-787 Ezekiel
9-780-805-490-152 Daniel
9-780-805-493-269 Hosea, Obadiah
9-780-805-493-344 Jonah, Zephaniah
9-780-805-490-657 Haggai, Malachi

New Testament

9-781-558-196-889 Matthew
9-780-805-490-718 Mark
9-780-805-490-046 Luke
9-781-558-196-933 John
9-781-558-196-919 Acts
9-780-805-490-053 Romans
9-780-805-493-252 1 Corinthians
9-780-805-493-351 2 Corinthians
9-781-558-196-902 Galatians
9-780-805-493-276 Ephesians

9-781-558-196-896 Philippians, Colossians,
Philemon
9-780-805-490-008 1 & 2 Thessalonians
9-781-558-196-926 1 & 2 Timothy, Titus
9-780-805-493-368 Hebrews
9-780-805-490-183 James
9-780-805-490-190 1 & 2 Peter & Jude
9-780-805-492-149 1, 2 & 3 John
9-780-805-490-176 Revelation

SHEPHERD'S NOTES CHRISTIAN CLASSICS

9-780-805-493-474 *Mere Christianity,*
C. S. Lewis
9-780-805-493-535 *The Problem of Pain/*
A Grief Observed,
C. S. Lewis
9-780-805-491-999 *The Confessions,*
Augustine
9-780-805-492-002 *Calvin's Institutes*
9-780-805-493-948 *Miracles,* C. S. Lewis

9-780-805-491-968 *Lectures to My Students,*
Charles Haddon
Spurgeon
9-780-805-492-200 *The Writings of Justin*
Martyr
9-780-805-493-450 *The City of God,*
Augustine
9-780-805-491-982 *The Cost of Discipleship,*
Bonhoeffer

SHEPHERD'S NOTES — BIBLE SUMMARY SERIES

9-780-805-493-771 Old Testament
9-780-805-493-788 New Testament

9-780-805-493-849 Life & Teachings of Jesus
9-780-805-493-856 Life & Letters of Paul

SHEPHERD'S NOTES
Christian Classics

Bonhoeffer's
Cost of Discipleship

HOLMAN
REFERENCE

NASHVILLE, TENNESSEE

Shepherd's Notes—Dietrich Bonhoeffer's *The Cost of Discipleship*
© 1998
by B&H Publishing Group
Nashville, Tennessee
All rights reserved
Printed in the United States of America

978-1-4627-6608-6

Dewey Decimal Classification: 241.5
Subject Heading: BONHOEFFER
Library of Congress Card Catalog Number: 98–21266

Library of Congress Cataloging-in-Publication Data

Ligon, Greg, 1962–
Dietrich Bonhoeffer's The cost of discipleship / Greg Ligon, editor.
        p.   cm. — (Shepherd's notes. Christian classics)
    Includes bibliographical references.
        1. Bonhoeffer, Dietrich, 1906–1945. Nachfolge.   2. Sermon on the mount—Criticism, interpretation, etc.   3. Christian life—Bekennende Kirche authors.   I. Title. II. Series.
    BT380.B674 1998
    241.5'3—dc21

                                                                98–21266
                                                                CIP

1 2 3 4 5 6 7 8   •   21 20 19 18 17

CONTENTS

Dear Reader:

Shepherd's Notes — *Classics Series* is designed to give you a quick, step-by-step overview of some of the enduring treasures of the Christian faith. They are designed to be used alongside the classic itself—either in individual study or in a study group.

Classics have staying power. Although they were written in a particular place and time and often in response to situations different than our own, they deal with problems, concerns, and themes that transcend time and place.

The faithful of all generations have found spiritual nourishment in the Scriptures and in the works of Christians from earlier generations. Martin Luther and John Calvin would not have become who they were apart from their reading Augustine. God used the writings of Martin Luther to move John Wesley from a religion of dead works to an experience at Aldersgate in which his "heart was strangely warmed."

It is an awesome sight—these streams of gracious influence flowing from generation to generation.

Shepherd's Notes—*Classics Series* will help you take the first steps in claiming and drawing strength from your spiritual heritage.

Shepherd's Notes is designed to bridge the gap between now and then and to help you understand, love, and benefit from the company of saints of an earlier time. Each volume gives you an overview of the main themes dealt with by the author and then walks with you step-by-step through the classic.

Enjoy!
In Him,

David R. Shepherd
Editor-in-Chief

How to Use This Book

DESIGNED FOR THE BUSY USER

Shepherd's Notes for Bonhoeffer's *Cost of Discipleship* is designed to provide an easy-to-use tool for gaining a quick overview of the major themes and the structure of *Cost of Discipleship*.

Shepherd's Notes are designed for laymen, pastors, teachers, small-group leaders and participants, as well as the classroom student.

DESIGNED FOR QUICK ACCESS

Persons with time restraints will especially appreciate the timesaving features built into *Shepherd's Notes*. All features are designed to work together to aid a quick and profitable encounter with *Cost of Discipleship*—to point the reader to sections in *Cost of Discipleship* where they may want to spend more time and go deeper.

Section-at-a-Glance. Cost of Discipleship is divided into 32 chapters. Section-at-a-Glance provides a listing of the chapters of that section.

Summary. Each section of *Cost of Discipleship* is summarized chapter by chapter.

Shepherd's Notes—Commentary. Following the summary of the section, a commentary is provided. This enables the reader to look back and see the major themes that make up that particular section.

Icons. Various icons in the margin provide information to help the reader better understand that part of the text. Icons include:

Shepherd's Notes Icon. This icon denotes the commentary on each section of the *Cost of Discipleship*.

Scripture Icon. Scripture verses often illuminate passages in *Cost of Discipleship*.

Historical Background Icon. Many passages in *Cost of Discipleship* are better understood in the light of historical, cultural, biographical, and geographical information.

Quotes Icon. This icon marks significant quotes from *Cost of Discipleship or* from other sources that illuminate the *Cost of Discipleship.*

 Points to Ponder Icon. These questions and suggestions for further thought will be especially useful in helping both individuals and groups see the relevance of *Cost of Discipleship* for our time.

INTRODUCTION

Adolf von Harnack

Dietrich Bonhoeffer, born in Breslau on February 4, 1906, was the son of Karl Bonhoeffer, a university professor and leading authority on psychiatry and neurology. His mother, Paula von Hase Bonhoeffer, was the daughter of an aristocratic German family. Many of his father's ancestors were theologians by vocation, and his mother's family also included a number of religious practitioners. Dietrich's maternal grandfather was chaplain to Kaiser Wilhelm and was ousted for disagreeing with the kaiser's political views. His mother's grandfather, Karl August von Hase, a historian by trade, was imprisoned for liberal theological views.

Dietrich's parents were known to be of exemplary character and very cultured. From his father he inherited much of his ability, as well as fairness and self-control. His mother was said to have contributed his understanding and sympathy toward others, his dedication to help the oppressed, and his unshakable tenacity.

The Bonhoeffer family was large. Dietrich was raised with three brothers and four sisters, one of which was his twin. In 1912, the family moved to Berlin into a neighborhood shared by Adolf von Harnack, a famous classical liberal theologian.

Dietrich's father, Karl, was closely associated with the University of Berlin, so at a very young age, Dietrich was impacted by a cultural and intellectual surrounding that was Christian, humanitarian, and liberal. It was likely this influence that shaped his decision to enter the field of religion at the age of fourteen. Though at

Adolf von Harnack (1851–1930) was a leading German Protestant theologian and historian, whose critical views were a major influence in late nineteenth- and early twentieth-century theology. He was educated at the universities of Dorpat and Leipzig. He was appointed professor extraordinary of church history at the University of Leipzig in 1876 and later held professorships at the universities of Giessen, Marburg, and Berlin. He served as president of the Evangelical Congress from 1902 to 1912 and as director of the Prussian National Library from 1905 to 1921. Harnack traced the evolution of the early church from biblical Christianity, which he claimed had been corrupted by the introduction of Greek metaphysics. He advocated a return to the simple faith of the original gospel; but his distrust of the institutional church, creeds, dogmas, and sacraments provoked the opposition of much more conservative scholars.

first disappointed, his father later commended this decision during the church's persecution under Hitler.

In a letter written during the persecution of the church by Hitler, Dietrich's father penned the following note: "When I heard that you intended to enter the pastorate as a boy, I thought that this was not the way that you should go, confining yourself to a corner of life. I thought at the time that such a removed and unreal existence as a pastor as I knew it from my uncle was too small; it was a pity that you would do that. Now, seeing the Church in a crisis that I never thought would be possible, I see that what you have chosen is very right."

During his seventeenth year, Dietrich entered Tübingen University. After a year of study at Tübingen and a summer in North Africa and Italy, Dietrich returned to Germany and entered the University of Berlin. There he was influenced by the teachings of Friedrich Schleiermacher, Albrecht Ritschl, Ernst Troeltsch, and Adolf von Harnack, all men who had played a significant role in shaping the theology at the university. In addition to the liberal tradition presented by these theologians, Bonhoeffer was impacted by his study of the contrasting theology of Karl Barth. Though he never studied under Barth, he eventually embraced many of his views and rejected the liberalism which had shaped his early theological convictions. In later years, Bonhoeffer worked with Barth in developing the Confessing Church in Germany.

In 1925, Bonhoeffer started work on his doctoral thesis with a focus on the nature of the church. His thesis, *Communion of the Saints*, framed much of his future study and theological

**Karl Barth
(1886–1968)**

A Swiss Protestant theologian, Barth is widely regarded as one of the most notable Christian thinkers of the twentieth century. He opposed the Hitler regime and was the chief author of the Barmen Declaration, which defined Christian opposition to National Socialist ideology and practice.

The principal emphasis in Barth's work, known as neoorthodoxy and crisis theology, was on the sinfulness of humanity, God's absolute transcendence, and the human inability to know God except through revelation. Barth saw the task of the church as that of proclaiming the "good word" of God and as serving as the "place of encounter" between God and humankind.

reflection. Two ideas were at the core of this work—the church as a human society and the church as the kingdom of God. Neither "ideal society" nor a "gathering of the gifted" describe the church. Rather, it is a product of God's action in history and existing human reality. As such, the church is "a communion of sinners" as well as "a communion of saints touched by the saving acts of Christ."

"A brilliant and theologically sophisticated young man."—Reinhold Niebuhr

In 1928, Bonhoeffer traveled to Barcelona and spent almost two years serving as an associate pastor to Germans living in the area. In 1930, at age twenty-four, he became a lecturer in systematic theology at the University of Berlin. After presenting his inaugural address in Berlin, he traveled to New York for an additional year of study as a Sloan Fellow at Union Theological Seminary and quickly gained a reputation as a fine scholar in the theological world.

Even at the height of his academic rigor, Bonhoeffer was committed to prophetic and pastoral ministry. During his stay in America, he was impacted by the dilemma of blacks. These experiences further shaped his conviction regarding the role of the church in social change. His deep desire was to bring Christianity into daily contact with the common community. He felt called to be a pastor as he returned to teach in Berlin. In addition to lecturing, he was known for engaging students outside the classroom for hours of dialogue. He served as student chaplain of The Technical University at Charlottenburg and prepared for confirmation a group of young boys living in the poorest section of Berlin. His love for academics was matched by a passion for ministry among the masses. Thus, in a true sense, he was a practical theologian.

In 1931, Bonhoeffer aligned himself with the World Alliance of Churches as one of three youth secretaries. This showed his commitment to the ecumenical movement, but was a risky move for his career because German nationalists were opposed to ecumenism. This involvement, he thought, was as an opportunity to work for world peace.

In a letter written to a girlfriend, Dietrich described a spiritual transformation, believed by most scholars to be his conversion, that occurred in 1931. In the letter he said: "Then something happened, something that has changed and transformed my life to the present day. For the first time I discovered the Bible. . . . I had often preached, I had seen a great deal of the Church, and talked and preached about it—but I had not yet become a Christian. . . . Also I had never prayed, or prayed only very little. For all my abandonment, I was quite pleased with myself. Then the Bible, and in particular the Sermon on the Mount, freed me from that. Since then everything has changed. I have felt this plainly, and so have other people about me. It was a great liberation. It became clear to me that the life of a servant of Jesus Christ must belong to the Church, and step by step it became clearer to me how far that must go."

On January 30, 1933, Adolf Hitler was installed as chancellor of Germany. A great realist, Bonhoeffer was one of the few who quickly understood, actually before Hitler came to power, that National Socialism was a godless attempt to make history on man's strength alone. Thus, from the beginning of the Third Reich, Dietrich was a dedicated adversary. Shortly after Hitler's rise to power was announced, he denounced this political system that placed authority in a

Adolf Hitler (1889–1945)

Adolf Hitler, a German political and government leader and one of the twentieth century's most powerful dictators, converted Germany into a fully militarized society, and launched World War II in 1939. Making anti-Semitism a keystone of his propaganda and policies, he built the Nazi party into a mass movement. For a time he dominated most of Europe and North Africa. He caused the slaughter of millions of Jews and other people whom he considered inferior.

person instead of an office, believing that this "grossly misled a nation and made the Führer its idol and god." Bonhoeffer's radio broadcast was cut short in the middle of this message.

Hitler quickly began to make moves to control the church. He ensured that the person of his choice, Chaplain Ludwig Müller, was elected to the primary adjudicatory role in the German evangelical church. "The 'German Christians'—those clergy and laymen who agreed with Hitler's racist views—gained control of the German church." Bonhoeffer, Barth, and other church leaders gathered at the meeting of the Barmen Synod on January 3–4, 1934. They drafted a statement clarifying the errors introduced into the church by the Nazis. This statement became the founding document of the Confessing Church.

In 1933, Dietrich Bonhoeffer went to London to serve as pastor to two German congregations. As he pastored, he also served as an unofficial ambassador, explaining the nature of the German church struggle. As Hitler's tyranny persisted, he spent many hours determining how best to resist. He had been impressed by Mahatma Ghandi's theories of passive resistance but struggled to determine how they applied in a Christian framework.

Friends in the Confessing Church convinced him to return to Germany and head an illegal Church Training College, the seminary of the Confessing Church. Young ministers willing to defy the Nazi ban on Confessing Church ordinations attended the school, organized first in Zingst and later moved to Finkenwalde. Bonhoeffer attempted to center life around the concept of Christian community. The school practiced a strict regimen of daily prayers and personal confession as Bonhoeffer lectured and discussed preaching and spiritual life. These experiences at Finkenwalde became the basis for his book *Life Together*.

In 1935, the Gestapo turned their attention to the seminary in 1935 and closed its doors in September 1937. This was the year Bonhoeffer published *The Cost of Discipleship*. Nevertheless, he continued to teach Confessing Church seminarians in a variety of locations until 1940 when the Gestapo stopped even this. The Confessing Church also struggled as many members, including their leader, Martin Niemöller, faced harassment and eventually imprisonment. In June 1939, friends brought Bonhoeffer to America to avoid further entanglement in the inevitable war. However, after only a short period, he returned to Germany convinced that he must.

In a letter to Reinhold Niebuhr, his American host, he outlined the following reasons for returning to Germany.

> Sitting here in Dr. Coffin's garden, I have had the time to think and to pray about my situation and that of my nation and to have God's will for me clarified. . . . I made a mistake in coming to America. I must live through this difficult period of our national history with the Christian people of Germany. I will have no right to participate in the reconstruction of Christian life in Germany after the war if I do not share the trials of this time with my people. My brethren in the Confessing Synod wanted me to go. They may have been right in urging me to do so, but I was wrong in going. Such a decision each man must make for himself. Christians in Germany will face the terrible alternative of either willing the defeat of their nation in order that Christian civ-

**Martin Niemöller
(1892–1984)**

Martin Niemöller was a German Lutheran pastor, whose anti-Nazi activities made him a symbolic figure in his church's struggle against Hitler. Niemöller was an organizer and leader of the Confessing Church, a group of German Protestant Christians who opposed Hitler's policies. On July 1, 1937, the Gestapo arrested him and incarcerated him, first at the concentration camp at Sachsenhausen and later at Dachau. They freed him in early 1945 as World War II was coming to an end. After the war, he became a leader in rebuilding the German Protestant church and in opposing atomic weapons and German rearmament. Niemöller served (1961–68) as one of the presidents of the World Council of Churches.

ilization may survive, or willing the victory of their nation and therefore destroying our civilization. I know which of these alternatives I must choose; but I cannot make that choice in security.

Bonhoeffer returned to Germany in July 1939, never regretting his decision.

In September 1939, Nazi forces attacked Poland and began their march through Belgium, Holland, Luxembourg, and France. In the summer of 1940, Bonhoeffer was banned from preaching but continued his work with the Confessing Church and with the political underground movement. He had a strong spiritual influence on the growing opposition in Germany and the attempts to overthrow Hitler. In the midst of all this, on January 17, 1943, Bonhoeffer became engaged to Maria von Wedemeyer. His and his sister's arrest in April 1943 cut short his marriage plans and resistance activities.

First imprisoned in Tegel, he was able to have much of his work—papers, letters, and poems—smuggled out through relationships developed with prison guards. His greatest concern during these days was obtaining permission to care for the sick and other fellow prisoners. In early October 1944, Bonhoeffer was moved from Tegel to the Gestapo's maximum-security prison on Prinz-Albrecht-Strasse in Berlin. In February 1945, as the Russian armies approached Berlin, he was again moved, this time to the infamous death camp at Buchenwald.

As the American forces advanced, Bonhoeffer and a group of prisoners were taken from the prison and driven along a German–controlled road to an old Bavarian schoolhouse where they were allowed to worship on April 8. This

Letter from Prison

"I am sure of God's hand and guidance. . . . You must never doubt that I am thankful and glad to go the way which I am being led. My past life is abundantly full of God's mercy, and, above all sin, stands the forgiving love of the Crucified" (August 23, 1944).

experience was described by Payne Best, a British secret service agent:

> Pastor Bonhoeffer held a little service and spoke to us in a manner which reached the hearts of all, finding just the right words to express the spirit of our imprisonment and the thoughts and resolutions which it had brought. He had hardly finished his last prayer when the door opened and two evil-looking men in civilian clothes came in and said: "Prisoner Bonhoeffer, get ready to come with us." Those words "come with us"—for all prisoners they had come to mean one thing only—the scaffold. We bade him good-bye—he drew me aside—"This is the end," he said. "For me, the beginning of life."

Bonhoeffer's Final Moments

"Through the half open door in one room of the huts, I saw Pastor Bonhoeffer, before taking off his prison garb, kneeling on the floor praying fervently to God. I was most deeply moved by the way this lovable man prayed, so devout and so certain that God heard his prayer. At the place of execution, he again said a short prayer and then climbed the steps to the gallows, brave and composed. His death ensued after a few seconds. In the almost fifty years that I worked as a doctor, I have hardly ever seen a man die so entirely submissive to the will of God."

Bonhoeffer was taken to the concentration camp in Flossenbürg where he was tried for treason, found guilty, and hanged.

In *The Cost of Discipleship*, Bonhoeffer had written, "When Christ calls a man, he bids him come and die," and, "Suffering, then, is the badge of true discipleship." Dietrich Bonhoeffer followed his Lord to the death faithfully wearing the badge of true discipleship.

IMPACT

Some have called Bonhoeffer a twentieth-century prophet. William Placher, in *A History of Christian Theology,* wrote, "Bonhoeffer was looking for a way to preach Christ in a world where all the old assumptions at the foundation of religion no longer seemed to make sense." *The Cost of Discipleship* has been seen by many as the foundation for his challenges to these assumptions. He called for an immediate obedience to the call of Jesus Christ. This "should not be misunderstood as a compromise of the priority of

Christ as mediator" or as a discrediting of the importance of the body of Christ, the church.

The immediacy is simply Bonhoeffer's call to renounce "false gods," to abandon anything that stands in the way of Jesus as the only path of salvation. This is the consistent impact that *The Cost of Discipleship* has had on its readers and the church through the years—the calling of men and women, and the whole church, back to the biblical foundations of relationship with Christ. It faithfully calls us to a real, transforming, costly discipleship.

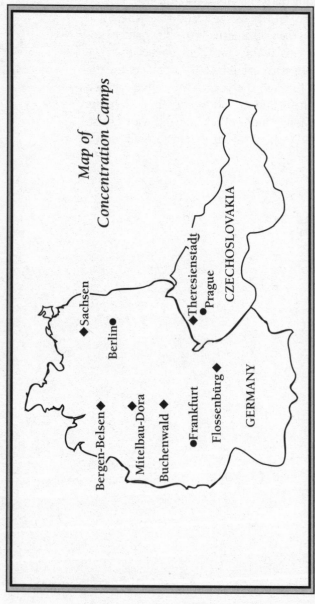

Map of Concentration Camps

Sachsen ◆
Berlin ●

Bergen-Belsen ◆
Mitelbau-Dora ◆
Buchenwald ◆

● Frankfurt
Flossenbürg ◆

Theresienstadt ◆
● Prague

GERMANY

CZECHOSLOVAKIA

Bonhoeffer was executed at Flossenbürg on April 9, 1945. Camps denoted by diamonds.

"When Christ calls a man, he bids him come and die" (ch. 4).

SECTION-AT-A-GLANCE

CHAPTER 1: COSTLY GRACE

Bonhoeffer opened this text with a powerful statement regarding what he identified as cheap grace. It is a chief enemy of the church. Cheap grace is "grace without price; grace without cost!" Many believe that the essence of grace is that the account has been paid in full in advance and therefore everything can be had for nothing. In the first chapter, a definition is outlined by painting a picture of the contrast between cheap and costly grace.

Cheap Grace

"Cheap grace is the deadly enemy of our Church."

1. "Cheap grace means grace as a doctrine, . . . a system."

This portrait of grace holds that an intellectual assent to an idea is sufficient to provide remission of sins. Grace is a cheap covering for sins; no repentance is necessary.

2. "Cheap grace means justification of sin without the justification of the sinner."

Cheap grace is the idea that "grace" did it all for me so I do not need to change my lifestyle. The believer who accepts the idea of "cheap grace" thinks he can continue to live like the rest of the world. Instead of following Christ in a radical way, the Christian lost in cheap grace thinks he can simply enjoy the consolations of his grace.

3. Cheap grace is:

How would you define the contrast between cheap and costly grace?

- preaching forgiveness without requiring repentance.
- baptism without church discipline.
- communion without confession.
- absolution without personal confession.
- grace without discipleship.
- grace without the cross.
- grace without Jesus.

We are not freed from the toils of sin by "cheap grace." This "cheap grace" rather than having been given by God, is the grace we give ourselves.

In contrast, real grace, "costly grace" challenges us "as a gracious call" to follow Christ Jesus.

The next part of this chapter takes the reader through a brief lesson in church history from the perspective of the understanding of grace. Bonhoeffer began with Peter's experience of grace. Peter received the call, "Follow me," two different times—at the beginning of his relationship with Jesus and at the end of his earthly relationship with Jesus. Between those two calls lay his life of discipleship. This life of discipleship included Peter's confession of Jesus as the Christ, another special visitation of God's grace. Grace and discipleship are inseparable in Peter's life because he "had received the grace which costs."

Christianity spread, becoming more popular and more secular; and as this happened, the realization that grace was costly gradually faded. "The world was Christianized, and grace became its common property." The monastic movement was perhaps the only place where the older, accurate vision of grace was maintained. Here men still left all for the sake of the call. In living the monastic life, people were a kind of "living protest" against both the secularization of the faith and cheap grace. However, monasticism, seen as an individual achievement, also came to be seen as lying outside the realm of what should be expected of a typical believer. This limited the applications of the commands of Jesus to a group of specialists and developed a layering of standards for obedience. Because of this, Bonhoeffer saw a paradoxical result in monasticism: While its mission was to preserve the realization of the costliness of grace, it gave instead final justification for the secularization of the church.

With the Reformation came a restoration of the gospel of pure, costly grace. In the Scriptures, God showed Luther that following Christ was not the achievement or merit of a select group. Rather it was commanded by God for all believers without distinction. Luther's return to the world from the cloistered life was a great blow to the world—perhaps the greatest blow since the days of early Christianity. The renunciation Luther made when going from the world to the cloister "was child's play" when compared to going back to the world. It was like a "frontal assault" to realize that the "only way to follow Jesus was by living in the world." What had been the achievement of a few was once again seen as a duty laid on every believer.

Some have misunderstood Luther's proclamation of grace alone for salvation, Bonhoeffer pointed out, taking it to mean that grace became a justification for disobeying the commands of Jesus. On the contrary, when Luther spoke of grace, he also always spoke of the reality that it cost him his own life; in receiving grace, he became subject to absolute obedience of Christ. Luther said that grace alone can save; but those words were always spoken in correlation with the obligation of discipleship, of obedience to Jesus.

The first chapter concludes with a review of the "costs" of cheap grace. He pointed to cheap grace as the cause for the problems of the organized church. Making grace available to all at too low a cost weakened the church. Bonhoeffer thought that the institutional church gave the Bible and the sacraments wholesale. He felt that the whole nation had been baptized, confirmed, and absolved without condition. Care for humanity caused Christians to give the holy to the scornful and unbelieving. Unending streams of grace were given, but Christ's narrow way was hardly ever heard.

Cheap grace also had an adverse impact on people's lives. Grace was intended to open the way to Christ, but cheap grace only closed it. In a like manner, grace was intended to call one to follow Jesus, but instead cheap grace only hardened individuals in their disobedience. Cheap grace simply barred the progress of believers, seducing them to believe that the mediocre level of living consistent with the world was life at its best. This cheap grace actually weakened and deceived men when they thought they were strong. In reality, they had lost the ability to live obedient lives as disciples.

Pure Grace

"Grace interpreted as a principle . . . grace at a low cost, is in its last resort simply a new law, which brings neither help nor freedom. Grace as a living word, . . . as our comfort in tribulation and as a summons to discipleship, costly grace is the only pure grace, which really forgives sin and gives freedom to the sinner" (ch. 1).

 COMMENTARY

The Cost of Discipleship begins with a section entitled "Grace and Discipleship." This section serves as one of several images painted throughout the book that depict the nature and character of discipleship. In later sections including "The Sermon on the Mount" and "The Messengers," Bonhoeffer added color and depth to the portrait he began in this initial section.

The first section, "Grace and Discipleship," begins with a chapter entitled "Costly Grace." In this chapter Bonhoeffer laid out his definition of *grace* through presentation of the contrast between what he termed, "cheap" and "costly" grace. As seen in the summary, cheap grace is grace without discipleship, communion without confession, baptism without church discipline, preaching forgiveness without requiring repentance. In addition, it is characterized by belief without obedience, hearing without doing, and intellectual assent without life commitment. Those who live a life of cheap grace "hold on" rather than "let go." A sense of casual acknowledgment results in an involvement that allows submission to the yoke of Christ to be held at arm's length. This understanding of cheap grace is vivified as it is compared to costly grace.

Costly grace is the grace of Christian discipleship. It is costly because it calls us to follow. It is costly because it costs our very lives. It is costly because it condemns sin. It is grace because when we are called to follow, the call is to follow Jesus. It is grace because although it costs our life, it is also the source of the only true and complete life. And it is grace because, although it condemns the sin, it justifies the sinner.

In the brief church history Bonhoeffer included in this chapter, he presented a succinct and clear understanding of the development in understanding of grace. He used Peter to depict the pure form of grace, grace that was costly and intended for all believers. Through the discussion of monasticism, he showed how this attempt by the church to protect itself from secularization ended up actually broadening the gap. The costly grace understood and experienced by the monks came to be seen, not as a model for all believers, but rather as an individual achievement required only by the spiritually elite. Finally, he argued that Luther and the Reformation had an accurate grasp of costly grace, but they were often misunderstood. In fact, the Reformation battle cry, "Not by works but by grace and through faith alone," became a justification for doing no works at all. And this led to a cheapening of grace.

In the final pages of chapter 1, Bonhoeffer lamented the manner by which cheap grace had resulted in the demise of the organized church as well as the spiritual lives of individuals. Cheap grace has served as an inoculation or more accurately, a vaccination. We have gotten just enough of Jesus to prevent us from catching the real thing. As a result we begin to feel secure even in the midst of godless living. We become unaware of our disobedience, and cheap grace provides us with a deceptive sense of strength. After all, we were told, our salvation has already been accomplished by the grace of God. The church and individuals will only recover the joy of discipleship when its cost is fully paid.

In this chapter, Bonhoeffer spoke of the "costs" of cheap grace for the church and for the individual. Do you see these same costs being paid today? In what way(s)?

Chapter 1 closes by stating the direction of the remainder of the text. Subsequent chapters will be pursued first with the confession that we are no longer standing in the path of true discipleship. Therefore, we must try to get back a true

In the next part of chapter 2, Bonhoeffer asserted that if one is to follow Jesus he or she must take certain steps. Step one separates the disciple from his previous existence. Step one takes the disciple out of the old situation and places him immediately into a new one where faith is possible.

What is identified as the "content" of discipleship?

In the paragraphs that follow this assertion, Bonhoeffer defended his position against those who might say this sounded as if he were promoting salvation through works. His defense is presented by means of the following points:

"First, faith, then obedience." Bonhoeffer certainly believed the Bible teaches that we are justified by faith. The problem comes when some try to come up with a sequential distinction between faith and, later, obedience. We must not separate the two. If this happens, then we must ask when obedience started, which is really to separate the two. If we are talking about justification, then they must be separated; but faith and obedience really share an essential unity. Faith is real only when we obey. Bonhoeffer believed that faith becomes faith when we obey.

Belief and Obedience

"Only he who believes is obedient, . . . only he who is obedient believes" (ch. 2).

"We must take a definite step." This means that we must concentrate on Jesus' call to come to Him, not on the work we do in responding to that call. We must first receive His call; and, then, we must respond. We *are* called by His grace. Actually, our first act, or step, of obedience is also an act of faith we take by believing Christ's words.

"Jesus says: 'First obey.'" The first act Jesus calls us to is to give up obstacles and attachments that separate us from God's will. This first step, in turn, leads us closer to Christ. Even if we don't believe, we should take the first step because Christ commands us to take it. We are not asked

What is considered the initial step of discipleship?

Matthew 19:16–22

"Now behold, one came and said to Him, 'Good Teacher, what good thing shall I do that I may have eternal life?' So He said to him, 'Why do you call Me good? No one is good but One, that is, God. But if you want to enter into life, keep the commandments.' He said to Him, 'Which ones?' Jesus said, '"You shall not murder," "You shall not commit adultery," "You shall not steal," "You shall not bear false witness," "Honor your father and your mother," and, "You shall love your neighbor as yourself."' The young man said to Him, 'All these things I have kept from my youth. What do I still lack?' Jesus said to him, 'If you want to be perfect, go, sell what you have and give to the poor, and you will have treasure in heaven; and come, follow Me.' But when the young man heard that saying, he went away sorrowful, for he had great possessions" (NKJV).

if we believe but ordered to obey then and there. This is the kind of response which will put us in a position where real faith becomes possible.

"Only those who believe obey, . . . and only those who obey believe." The soul of the believer knows that when we believe we will obey and when we obey we believe. If we believe but do not obey, the believer is laid open to the danger of cheap grace. If we obey but don't believe, we are laid open to the danger of salvation through works.

Bonhoeffer next discussed the story of the rich young ruler as recorded in Matthew 19:16–22.

The young man asked a serious question regarding salvation. He fully expected to receive a well-thought-out disclosure of significant proportions. He received instead a command to obey. He was told to stop his questioning and to obey the will of God. But the young man responded to Jesus' command with an evasive question with regard to which commandment he should obey. Bonhoeffer believed that the response revealed a model often used by Satan: If we keep bringing up questions, we might escape having to obey altogether. Twice now Jesus faced him with the truth. His only option was to obey. Yet he is still not ready and asked: "All these I have kept. What do I still lack?"

Jesus, of course, realized how hopelessly the young person had closed his mind to God's Word. He was not willing to obey because his heart raged against God's commandment. Yet Jesus loved the young man and wanted to help. Jesus' last word to the young man was: "If thou wilt be perfect, go, and sell that thou hast, and give it to the poor, and thou shalt have treasure in heaven: and *come and follow me*" (KJV). The way to life eternal is to respond in faith and obedience to the call of Jesus, no ifs, ands, or buts. Standing face-to-face with Jesus the only question is, Will he obey? Bonhoeffer believed that the life of discipleship is not "hero-worship" directed to "a good master," but obedience to God through His Son.

 ## COMMENTARY

Central to Bonhoeffer's theology of discipleship is the importance of call. He began chapter 2, "The Call to Discipleship," with the passage in Mark that details Jesus' calling of Levi. He articulated the fact that the immediate sequence of Jesus' call and Levi's response are a matter of crucial importance, asserting that the cause behind the immediate following of a call is a response to Jesus Christ Himself. Indeed that is the essence of the call to discipleship.

The content of discipleship is simply following the call of Jesus. In fact, discipleship in this chapter is defined as "exclusive attachment" to the person of Jesus. This definition reveals also the importance of the personal nature of discipleship. The call that establishes the way of discipleship is the call to follow a person, Jesus. It is not a call to follow some abstract theology or doctrinal statement. Christianity without the living Christ is inevitably Christianity without discipleship, and Christianity without discipleship is always Christianity without Christ.

Through the passage from Luke's Gospel, Bonhoeffer used the imperfections of three "would be disciples" to clarify what is central to a true call to discipleship. The first would-be disciple

21

offered to follow Jesus, the second allowed circumstances to stand in the way of following the call, and the third attempted to establish his own terms for the journey of discipleship. The first was not truly called, the second allowed something to stand as a barrier between himself and Jesus, and the third's self-planned discipleship program reduced discipleship to the level of human understanding. The true disciple when called, does not allow anything to come between himself and Jesus, and does not presume to know what he needs along his journey toward maturity in Christ.

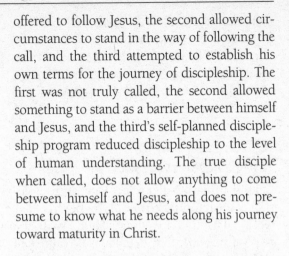

Which one of the above three attempts at discipleship do you most identify with and why?

This chapter concludes with the assertion that the call to discipleship is followed by a first step. This first step cuts the disciple off from his previous existence. The call to follow at once produces a new situation. To stay in the old situation makes discipleship impossible. The first step places the disciple in the situation where faith is possible. This truth is illustrated by means of the story of the rich young ruler as presented in Matthew 19. Jesus loved the young man and was calling him, but the rich young ruler was not willing to take the required step. He had come with a question regarding salvation and had hoped to receive a bit of advice from a wise master.

Instead he found himself faced with an answer that was embodied by the wise Master. This answer required a response, a first step. In his case, it was a step that involved selling all that he had (giving up all that he depended on) so that he might become a true follower of Jesus. For him, it was too large a step to take. Closely tied to Bonhoeffer's discipleship tenet of "exclusive attachment" to Christ is the position of the importance of obedience as presented in the following chapter, "Single-Minded Obedience."

CHAPTER 3: SINGLE-MINDED OBEDIENCE

Chapter 3 begins with this powerful quote: "Only one thing was required in each case—to rely on Christ's word, and cling to it as offering greater security than all the securities in the world." We are reminded that the forces which try to come between the word of Christ and our obedience are just as powerful today. Satan today, as he did then, sometimes uses reason, conscience, responsibility, and even piety to stand in the way. Even the law and "scriptural authority" itself were used as obstacles to keep people from responding to the call of single-minded obedience to God, to protect us from the extremes of "antinomianism" and "enthusiasm." But Jesus made it abundantly clear that these were barriers being used to come between Him and us, that obedience was the real issue. His call was the living Word of God and required single-minded obedience.

Bonhoeffer continued in his review of the understandings of obedience in his day. He thought if his contemporaries read the Bible, they would probably say something like: "Yes, Jesus does command us to obey, but He would never want us to take His commands in a legalistic way. What He really wants is for us to have faith." Bonhoeffer said this is excusing ourselves from single-minded obedience with the pretext that this is legalism when what Jesus actually preferred is obedience in faith. A series of similar examples is presented, each revealing an attempt to evade the obligation of single-minded obedience.

One Thing Required

"When he was challenged by Jesus to accept a life of voluntary poverty, the rich man knew he was faced with the simple alternative of obedience or disobedience. When Levi was called from the receipt of custom and Peter from his nets, there was no doubt that Jesus meant business. Both of them were to leave everything and follow. . . . Only one thing was required in each case—to rely on Christ's word, and cling to it as offering greater security than all the securities in the world."

Antinomianism and Enthusiasms

The *Handbook of Theological Terms* offers the following discussion regarding antinomianism: "On the grounds that the Christian is saved by grace and not by works or moral effort, some Christians have claimed that the saved man is free from all moral obligations or principles." John Wesley, founder of the Methodist Church, identified enthusiasts as those prone to giving undue weight to extraordinary experiences. "Two or three began to take their own imaginations for impressions from God, and thence to suppose they should never die; and these, labouring to bring others into the same opinion, occasioned much noise and confusion."

It is affirmed that, indeed, in the end what really matters is faith in Jesus as the Son of God, not what a man does. There is a sense in which the commandments seem to present us with a paradox (a seemingly contradictory statement that may nonetheless be true) at times, but this must never lead us to abandon the single-minded understanding of His commandments. There can be no substitute for the call of Jesus and a response on our parts of single-minded obedience. This, after all, is how we are brought into a situation where real faith is possible. There is no other conclusion but that when we eliminate single-minded obedience we are opting for the cheap grace of self-justification rather than the costly grace to which Jesus calls us.

This chapter closes with a reminder that single-minded obedience should not be confused with human merit. "Obedience to the call of Jesus never lies within our own power." The act of giving away all of our possessions is not in itself the obedience Jesus demands. In fact, even such a seeming "sacrifice" might be exactly the opposite of obedience to Him. Indeed, in this we may in reality be choosing a way of life for ourselves, believing it to be some "Christian ideal." Bonhoeffer thought that in the act of giving everything we have away we could still be choosing an act of allegiance to ourselves. This, of course, would not set us free from self but would enslave us all the more. "The step into the situation where faith is possible is not an offer which we can make to Jesus, but always his gracious offer to us. Only when the step is taken in this spirit is it admissible."

COMMENTARY

Understanding discipleship begins with obedience. This obedience is characterized by terms such as *immediate*, *total*, *concrete*, and in this chapter, *single-mindedness*. Bonhoeffer's struggle with ego and desire to dominate and exercise power over others shaped the question, How can I be saved from my self-seeking desire for power? This is addressed in the commanding picture of Christ he presented. Christ demands obedience, exclusive attachment and participation in the cross (chapter 4)—all elements of the costly grace Bonhoeffer discussed at the beginning of this text and which he believed to be central to Christian discipleship.

What are the academic excuses offered regarding the lack of "single-minded obedience"? What is the distinction between single-minded obedience and human merit?

A significant portion of chapter 3 is spent revealing the means by which men and women evade the demands of single-minded obedience. It is suggested that this is absurd, and a clarifying illustration is offered. Bonhoeffer related that when a father sends a child to bed at night there is no question about what is to be done. But what if the child has "picked up a smattering of pseudo-theology?" The child might reason that what father is really concerned about is that he fears I am tired. But the child continues, I can stop being tired by going out to play. "Thus, father really means for me to go out to play." But, said, Bonhoeffer, what child who tried such would not be met with language he could not fail to understand; i.e., punishment. Should we really, then, treat Jesus' commands differently than the plain language so clearly intended. In fact, when we do so, we exchange single-minded obedience for nothing less than downright disobedience.

What forces impose themselves between the word of Jesus and the response of obedience in your life?

This chapter closes with a return to the defense that costly discipleship is not to be confused with human excellence or ability. Indeed, obedience to Jesus' call is from His initiative, His grace, His power, and never our own. It calls us to be utterly dependent on the one who calls—Jesus Christ.

CHAPTER 4: DISCIPLESHIP AND THE CROSS

Mark 8:31–38

"And He began to teach them that the Son of Man must suffer many things, and be rejected by the elders and chief priests and scribes, and be killed, and after three days rise again. He spoke this word openly. Then Peter took Him aside and began to rebuke Him. But when He had turned around and looked at His disciples, He rebuked Peter, saying, 'Get behind Me, Satan! For you are not mindful of the things of God, but the things of men.' When He had called the people to Himself, with His disciples also, He said to them, 'Whoever desires to come after Me, let him deny himself, and take up his cross, and follow Me. For whoever desires to save his life will lose it, but whoever loses his life for My sake and the gospel's will save it. For what will it profit a man if he gains the whole world, and loses his own soul? Or what will a man give in exchange for his soul? For whoever is ashamed of Me and My words in this adulterous and sinful generation, of him the Son of Man also will be ashamed when He comes in the glory of His Father with the holy angels" (NKJV).

In this passage, it is pointed out that the call to follow is closely connected to Jesus' passion.

The early portion of the chapter presents a review of the truth that Jesus had to suffer and be rejected in order that the Scriptures would be fulfilled. Bonhoeffer went on to state that Jesus made it clear that the *must* of suffering applied to His disciples no less than to Himself. Just as Jesus had to suffer, so His disciples must share in this suffering and rejection, perhaps even in his crucifixion. One cannot be a disciple unless one adheres to the person of Jesus. When Jesus began to teach this truth to His disciples, He presented another point of decision: "If any man will come after me, let him deny himself" (Matt. 16:24, KJV). A Christian must deny self. This means to be aware of Christ and not of self. In this we must know that He leads and we are His only by keeping close to Him. Only when we become selfless, unaware of the pain of our own cross, are we ready to bear the cross for the sake of Christ. Rather than being a tragedy, such suffering—enduring the cross—for the Christian is in reality the fruit of "exclusive allegiance to Jesus Christ." Such suffering, when it comes, is for the sake of and cause of Christ.

What does it mean for you to deny yourself and follow Christ?

The remainder of this chapter presents a variety of characteristics associated with the cross.

- The cross is a part of every true disciple's life.
- The first suffering all Christians must suffer is the call to abandon all worldly attachments.
- Carrying the cross involves the suffering associated with being tempted; and since every day the believer is tempted, every day the believer must suffer for Jesus Christ's sake.

The closing pages of chapter 4 present the concept that the cross calls us to *bear* the cross.

Suffering

"Suffering, then, is the badge of true discipleship."

Jesus modeled for us the meaning of *communion*. As His suffering maintained His communion with the Father, so our endurance is necessary for followers of Christ to maintain communion with God. If we deny the burden we are called to carry, we will find that "the yoke of our self" is an even heavier one to carry. The seeming irony is that only under Jesus' yoke are we certain of His presence and communion and able to carry any yoke at all.

 COMMENTARY

Another central tenet in Bonhoeffer's theology of discipleship is participation in the cross of Christ. This is the focus of chapter 4, "Discipleship and the Cross." Participation in the cross includes suffering, rejection, burden bearing, and self-denial. Taking up the cross begins with the abandonment of the world and requires a daily self-denial not measured by "a series of isolated acts of mortification or asceticism" but rather an awareness "only of Christ and no more of self."

In the explanation of discipleship and the cross, we return to the definition of *discipleship* first presented in chapter 2. *Discipleship* means adherence to the person of Jesus, and *attachment to Jesus* means submission to the law of Christ, which is the law of the cross. The law of the cross calls for the denial of self and the choice to take up the cross given by God. Bonhoeffer is quick to remind that enduring the cross is not a tragedy but rather the suffering which is the fruit of an exclusive allegiance to Jesus Christ.

CHAPTER 5: DISCIPLESHIP AND THE INDIVIDUAL

Luke 14:26

"If anyone comes to Me and does not hate his father and mother, wife and children, brothers and sisters, yes, and his own life also, he cannot be My disciple" (NIV).

This chapter opens with the assertion that "through the call of Jesus men become individuals." Again, it is no decision of their own but Christ's calling that makes them individual. All receive an individual call; but because a man fears isolation, he attempts to align himself with others and their physical environment. Men try to build a barrier which will prevent a decision having to be made. Men are not willing to stand alone before Jesus. But neither parents, family, even nationality or "tradition, can protect a man at the moment of his call."

The necessity of this individualism is again the call of Christ to come apart from the world. He wants to be at the center of our world. The break with the world is "identical with the acknowledgment of Christ as the Son of God the Mediator." When we receive the call of Jesus, we realize that our present physical world has been built on an illusion. When we receive His call, we realize that even in such relationship as father and son, husband and wife, stands Christ the Mediator, and no other relationship can be as important as the one with Christ the Mediator.

COMMENTARY

What is mean by the following statement: "Just as Christ is Christ only in the virtue of His suffering and rejection, so the disciple is a disciple only in so far as he shares his Lord's suffering and rejection and crucifixion"? What is meant by, "People become individuals through the call of Jesus"?

In this final chapter of Section I, "Discipleship and the Individual," the belief is defended that through the call of Jesus, men are made to be individuals. This belief points again to the centrality of Christ. This point is used as the foundation for discussion concerning belief that Christ must be the Mediator not only between God and man but also between individuals.

Throughout this first section, discipleship is rooted in costly grace, adherence to the person of Christ, single-minded obedience, and sharing in the suffering of the cross of Christ, all initiated by the words of Jesus, "Follow me." This discipleship is a unique experience. Geffrey Kelly, in his book *Liberating Faith*, stated it this way:

> This call to discipleship is a unique experience of both liberating grace and Christ's commands, devoid of legalism, yet binding. "It is," Bonhoeffer observed, "nothing else than bondage to Jesus Christ alone, completely breaking through every program, every ideal, every set of laws." Discipleship then, is a complete attachment to Christ's person. One must be wholly directed toward Christ, looking neither to law nor to personal piety nor to the world for fulfillment. The following of Christ exacts a single-mindedness in which one's heart and ambitions are set on Christ alone.

SECTION II: THE SERMON ON THE MOUNT

- - - -

"In Christ crucified and in his people the 'extraordinary' becomes reality."

SECTION-AT-A-GLANCE

CHAPTER 6: THE BEATITUDES

This chapter is devoted to a discussion of the Beatitudes. At the onset, a picture is painted of the scene in which the Beatitudes were presented. Jesus, the crowds, and the disciples are

Matthew 5:1–12

And seeing the multitudes, He went up on a mountain, and when He was seated His disciples came to Him. Then He opened His mouth and taught them, saying: "Blessed are the poor in spirit, For theirs is the kingdom of heaven. Blessed are those who mourn, For they shall be comforted. Blessed are the meek, For they shall inherit the earth. Blessed are those who hunger and thirst for righteousness, For they shall be filled. Blessed are the merciful, For they shall obtain mercy. Blessed are the pure in heart, For they shall see God. Blessed are the peacemakers, For they shall be called sons of God. Blessed are those who are persecuted for righteousness' sake, For theirs is the kingdom of heaven. Blessed are you when they revile and persecute you, and say all kinds of evil against you falsely for My sake. "Rejoice and be exceedingly glad, for great is your reward in heaven, for so they persecuted the prophets who were before you" (NKJV).

gathered on a mountainside. The crowds see Jesus with the disciples, men who, until the recent call, had themselves been identified with those that made up the crowd. The disciples saw the crowds from whose midst they had come. And Jesus saw the disciples.

Jesus called His disciples "blessed" as He spoke to those who had responded to His call. It is the call itself, said Bonhoeffer, that made them poor, afflicted, and hungry. The disciples were called "blessed" because they obeyed Jesus' call. For this call, and the promise of Jesus, they were ready to suffer even poverty and rejection. This alone justifies the Beatitudes.

The remainder of chapter 6 outlines the Beatitudes with associated brief commentary.

Hardship is the circumstance of the disciples in every area of life. They have no security, no possessions, no spiritual power, no experience or knowledge. They have given up everything for His sake. In this state they are blessed, for theirs is the kingdom of heaven.

Matthew 5:4 means to do without peace and prosperity as the world knows it. Jesus wants us to refuse to be "in tune" with the world or to adapt ourselves to its standards. Believers mourn for the world and its idolatry.

The meek are those that "renounce every right of their own and live for the sake of Jesus Christ." They resolve to leave their rights and the protection thereof to God, and in turn they shall inherit the earth.

In addition to the renunciation of rights, disciples renounce their own righteousness. As a result, along the path of discipleship, they will become hungry and thirsty—"longing for the forgiveness of all sin, for complete renewal." They receive, in turn, the gift of complete satisfaction.

The merciful are those that have an "irresistible love for the down-trodden, the sick, the wretched, the wronged. . . . They are glad to incur reproach, for they know that then they are blessed."

The pure in heart are "those who have surrendered their hearts completely to Jesus that he may reign in them alone. . . . They are wholly absorbed by the contemplation of God."

Peacemakers are those who "keep the peace by choosing to endure suffering themselves rather than inflict it on others."

"The world will be offended at them, and so the disciples will be persecuted for righteousness' sake. Not recognition, but rejection, is the reward they get from the world for their message and works."

 **COMMENTARY**

In Section I, "Grace and Discipleship", Bonhoeffer laid the groundwork for his understanding of discipleship, namely the requirement of "costly grace." In this middle portion of the text (Section II), "The Sermon on the Mount," he added further definition to this understanding. The commentary he presented on these well-known chapters of the Gospel of Matthew reveals his belief that "the Sermon on the Mount is there for the purpose of being done." He made clear that the only appropriate conduct of men before God is the

Beatitudes

For the next month, spend some time each morning reflecting on one of the Beatitudes. Create some journal entries and spend some time in prayer regarding the characteristics articulated in the Beatitudes.

Sola Fide

Sola Fide is Latin for salvation by faith alone. "Salvation, according to Lutheran teaching, does not depend on worthiness or merit but is a gift of God's sovereign grace. Lutherans believe that faith, understood as trust in God's steadfast love, is the only appropriate way for human beings to respond to God's saving initiative. Thus, 'salvation by faith alone' became the distinctive and controversial slogan of Lutheranism. Opponents claimed that this position failed to do justice to the Christian responsibility to do good works, but Lutherans have replied that faith must be active in love and that good works follow from faith as a good tree produces good fruit."

doing of His will and that Matthew 5–7 is a clear picture of what that "doing" involves.

This second of the three works on discipleship contained in *The Cost of Discipleship* dispenses with the critical discussions, which have been the focus of other interpreters, and approaches the Sermon as a "concrete expression of discipleship that required 'doing' rather than 'interpreting.' Thus, in contrast to his times and since, his primary concern was the 'practical' rather than the 'theological' dimension of the Sermon studies. His exposition so strongly emphasizes the life and conduct of the Christian as set forth in the Sermon by Jesus that he could . . . be accused of surrendering his Lutheran heritage of sola fide for salvation by works of obedience."

Section II is divided into three parts, each covering a chapter of the Gospel of Matthew contained in the Sermon on the Mount. Matthew 5 is discussed in the first part of Section II entitled "Of the 'Extraordinariness' of the Christian Life." "In Christ crucified and in his people the 'extraordinary' becomes reality." The hallmark of the Christian life is this being "extraordinary." Chapters 6 through 13 detail what this characteristic of being "extraordinary" involves—including blessedness, a visible life, a "better righteousness," reconciliation, absolute purity, truthfulness, nonviolence, and a love for enemies.

As portrayed in the diagram, each of these qualities involved in being extraordinary is bound to the Cross. Again, we are pointed to the centrality of the Cross in the life of the disciple.

Chapter 6 speaks of the "blessedness" of the disciples. As Matthew 5 begins, we see Jesus on the mountainside teaching the disciples within view of the crowd. And in this setting, Jesus called his disciples "blessed."

The word *blessed* is especially appropriate in this context where it "describes the nearly incomprehensible happiness of those who participate in the kingdom announced by Jesus. Rather than happiness in its mundane sense, it refers to the deep inner joy of those who have long awaited the salvation promised by God and who are now beginning to experience its fulfillment." In his commentary, *Matthew for Today*, Michael Green indicated that *blessed* means, "made happy by God."

The disciples are blessed because they have answered the call and promise of Jesus. They are blessed because they are "poor in spirit"; they have given up everything for the sake of the call. They are blessed because they "mourn"; for the world in its lost state. They are blessed because they are "meek"; leaving their rights and protection to God. They are blessed because they "hunger"; for perfect union with the Father. They are blessed because they are "merciful"; having an irresistible love for the downtrodden. They are blessed because they are "pure in heart"; surrendered completely to Jesus. They are blessed because they are "peacemakers"; enduring suffering rather than inflicting it on others. They are blessed because they are "persecuted"; rejected for their message and works. Again, they are blessed because they have answered Jesus' call.

CHAPTER 7: THE VISIBLE COMMUNITY

The recipients of these words are the same as those who received the Beatitudes—those who have been called to follow Jesus, living the life of grace. But now, instead of blessed, they are

Blessed

The true background for the word *blessed* is found in the Old Testament. It is often used as a translation of a Hebrew word meaning "deeply happy."

Blessed

In what ways have you experienced God's blessing?

Matthew 5:13–16

"You are the salt of the earth; but if the salt loses its flavor, how shall it be seasoned? It is then good for nothing but to be thrown out and trampled underfoot by men. You are the light of the world. A city that is set on a hill cannot be hidden. Nor do they light a lamp and put it under a basket, but on a lampstand, and it gives light to all who are in the house. Let your light so shine before men, that they may see your good works and glorify your Father in heaven" (NKJV).

referred to as the salt—"the most indispensable necessity of life. The disciples, that is to say, are the highest good, the supreme value which the earth possesses, for without them it cannot live." The disciples are instructed to take a look at the earth whose salt they have become through their exclusive attachment to Jesus.

Another reflection made regarding the nature of salt with reference to the disciples is that both for the sake of the earth as well as for its own sake, salt must remain salty. The community of believers must be faithful to the mission Jesus has given to it. In addition, Jesus said, "You are the salt of the earth." This is not an option, something the disciples decide for themselves.

The call of Jesus also requires the disciples to be the "light of the world." Their activity is to be visible as well as unseen. They cannot be other than a light because they have been called. If they are not a light, it is a clear sign that they have not been called. If our community and activities as believers were not visible, we would not be disciples. "Flight into the invisible is a denial of the call."

But it is in the light of the call of Christ that the works of believers must be seen. The good works are to speak out and draw men to Jesus, not to the people who do the works. This is most important. In fact, what could be a better test for the "purity of the work" than that it draws men first and foremost to Christ. Christ shines so clearly as to make obscure the disciple who does the work on behalf of his Lord and Savior. The works done are really the ones created in the disciples when He called us "to be the light of the world under the shadow of his cross." All good works stand beneath the cross of Jesus Christ. This is what we, as disciples, must make visible.

COMMENTARY

Chapter 7 outlines the visible nature of the disciple's life. This is done through the reference to salt and light metaphors Jesus used in verses Matthew 5:13–16. "You are the salt of the earth" suggests at least three things: purity, preservation, and flavor. Salt in the Roman world symbolized purity—no doubt from the process of using sea water and the sun to acquire the salt. Salt was used to preserve meat and "salt loses itself in service to the object that is being salted . . . which is the third aspect of the meaning of this symbol— flavor." The metaphor is used as a tool to ground the disciples in reality. They had an earthly task to perform and must not fall into the trap of thinking only of heaven.

"You are the light of the world." Here is further support for the notion that the life of the disciple is to be visible. Since the disciples are the light of the world, their good works should be seen. These works bear the mark of the Cross. In short, the disciple's visibility points to the source of their call—Jesus and the Cross.

CHAPTER 8: THE RIGHTEOUSNESS OF CHRIST

It is not surprising that the disciples thought the law had been voided when Jesus made promises such as made in Matthew 5:17–20. "For these promises reversed all popular notions of right and wrong, and pronounced a blessing on all that was accounted worthless." After all, as

When speaking of Jesus' call to be light in darkness, Bonhoeffer stated that those that flee from the light—hide their light under a bushel—are denying the call to discipleship. Bonhoeffer suggested that the bushel in a man's life might be the "fear of men, or perhaps the deliberate conformity to the world for some ulterior motive." What are the "bushels" you are tempted to hide your light beneath?

Matthew 5:17–20

"Do not think that I came to destroy the Law or the Prophets. I did not come to destroy but to fulfill. For assuredly, I say to you, till heaven and earth pass away, one jot or one tittle will by no means pass from the law till all is fulfilled. Whoever therefore breaks one of the least of these commandments, and teaches men so, shall be called least in the kingdom of heaven; but whoever does and teaches them, he shall be called great in the kingdom of heaven. For I say to you, that unless your righteousness exceeds the righteousness of the scribes and Pharisees, you will by no means enter the kingdom of heaven" (NKJV).

Bonhoeffer had shown in Section I, *discipleship* meant adherence to Jesus Christ and Him alone. Where does obedience to the Old Testament Law fit in this picture of costly discipleship? It became clear to the early disciples that they were bound to Christ and not the Old Testament Law.

The "fundamental presupposition of the whole Sermon on the Mount" is that the Christ came to fulfill Old Testament Law. Jesus clearly stated his perfect union with the will of the God of Abraham, Isaac, and Jacob. One cannot fulfill the Law apart from communion with God. Jesus Christ alone fulfilled the Law because only He lived in perfect communion with God. "But if Jesus comes between the disciples and the Law, he does so not to release them from the duties it imposes, but to validate his demand that they should fulfil it. Just because they are bound to him, they must obey the Law as he does."

This passage in Matthew also indicates that the righteousness of the disciples will exceed that of the Pharisees. What is the derivation of this difference? Bonhoeffer said that the Pharisees never seemed to realize that the Law must be taught and not obeyed. They wanted to be doers of the law. Righteousness for them was to model behavior exactly on their understanding of the demands of the law, even though their obedience was always imperfect.

The disciples had the advantage because between them and the Old Testament law stands Jesus who perfectly fulfilled the Law. The disciple can live in communion with Christ who fulfilled the Law. They are faced with one whose demands have already been satisfied. Righteousness, for the Christian, is not a duty owed but a communion with God because of Christ.

COMMENTARY

In chapter 8, the next quality of the extraordinary life of the disciple is described as *"better righteousness."* This description is framed in a discussion of the authority of the Law. Bonhoeffer pointed out that Jesus clearly requires disciples to obey the Old Testament Law. In fact, this required obedience to the Law is the distinguishing mark of the better righteousness. The disciple's righteousness is better (than the Pharisees) because he is, in fact, able to obey the Law perfectly. How? The disciple is able to perfectly fulfill the law because between the disciples and the Law stands one—Jesus—who has perfectly fulfilled it. "Better righteousness" means following Christ in a real and active faith in Jesus' righteousness. Jesus has given us a new law, the law of Christ.

CHAPTER 9: THE BROTHER

When Jesus said: "But I say to you" He summed up the whole meaning of the Law. Jesus, as the Son of God, was the Author and Giver of the Law. Therefore, only those who comprehend the Law as the Word of Christ can fulfill it. Jesus first commended the law that prohibits murder and gives the disciples a level of responsibility in caring for their "brother." Here *brother* means more than family and even more than fellow Christian. For the Christian, there can be no one that does not qualify as brother or as neighbor, unless the Lord should so judge.

Jesus explained that the commandment, "Thou shall not kill," means that even anger is a

Righteousness

"The righteousness of the disciples can never be a personal achievement; it is always a gift."

What did Jesus mean in Matthew 5 when He said, "You are the salt of the earth. . . . You are the light of the world"? To whom was He addressing these statements? What does it mean to be salt and light in today's culture?

Matthew 5: 21–26

"You have heard that it was said to those of old, 'You shall not murder, and whoever murders will be in danger of the judgment.' But I say to you that whoever is angry with his brother without a cause shall be in danger of the judgment. And whoever says to his brother, 'Raca!' shall be in danger of the council. But whoever says, 'You fool!' shall be in danger of hell fire. Therefore if you bring your gift to the altar, and there remember that your brother has something against you, leave your gift there before the altar, and go your way. First be reconciled to your brother, and then come and offer your gift. Agree with your adversary quickly, while you are on the way with him, lest your adversary deliver you to the judge, the judge hand you over to the officer, and you be thrown into prison. Assuredly, I say to you, you will by no means get out of there till you have paid the last penny" (NKJV).

violation of the boundary of a "brother's" life. Anger itself is an attack on a brother's life because it interferes with the life and, by its very nature, aims at the brother's destruction. When a person gets angry and swears at a brother, or insults him in public, or slanders him, according to Bonhoeffer, that man is guilty of murder and so renounces his connection to God. By so doing, a barrier is erected between himself and his brother and his God. We must be reconciled with our brother to follow Jesus and worship God.

COMMENTARY

The fourth component of the "extraordinary" life of the disciple is *reconciliation*. This fourth piece is discussed in chapter 9 by expanding on the Old Testament commandment prohibiting murder. Jesus' "expansion" of the commandment to include anger is revealed. Bonhoeffer believed that murdering your brother in your heart, which is what anger is, is a transgression of God's law. Such puts a person in danger of judgment. To Jesus, our inner attitude is of ultimate importance. Jesus' teaching on this matter is radical and "apparently allows for no exception."

The disciple exhibits his "extraordinariness" by resolving anger through reconciliation. The barriers between a man and his brother and a man and God, which are erected by anger, are torn down through reconciliation.

CHAPTER 10: WOMAN

The Christian must exercise control over desire because even the desire of the moment is a barrier to discipleship. Bonhoeffer said that such desire can bring the whole body into hell and we are, in effect, selling our Christian birthright for a mess of pottage. When we submit to these desires, we show that we lack faith in Jesus. This is a clear case of not trusting God but of wanting the "tangible fruits of desire." This will cause us to forsake our discipleship and loose contact with Jesus. In reality, lust is unbelief and must be renounced at all costs. In this regard, no sacrifice which allows us to overcome lust is too great.

Jesus' restrictions are not intolerable. Christ bids us to look at Him, and in so doing our gaze will always be pure, even when looking at persons of the opposite sex.

COMMENTARY

In chapter 10, the fifth element of exemplary Christian living is presented— *absolute purity*. This quality is discussed in the context of the seventh commandment against adultery. Here again it is not merely the act which is condemned, but the attitude from which it comes. Bonhoeffer cut to the heart of the matter in his description of lust as unbelief and his assertion that we often prefer the "tangible fruits of desire" to trust in Christ. He is quick to point out that these attitudes and their associated actions cause us to "fall from . . . discipleship and lose touch with Jesus."

This chapter closes with an interpretation of Jesus' direction to pluck out an eye or cut off a hand if either causes you to disobey. Literally no sacrifice is too great if it conquers that which cuts us off from Jesus. Michael Green supported Bonhoeffer through his statement: "He [Jesus] is

Matthew 5: 27–32

"You have heard that it was said to those of old, 'You shall not commit adultery.' But I say to you that whoever looks at a woman to lust for her has already committed adultery with her in his heart. If your right eye causes you to sin, pluck it out and cast it from you; for it is more profitable for you that one of your members perish, than for your whole body to be cast into hell. And if your right hand causes you to sin, cut it off and cast it from you; for it is more profitable for you that one of your members perish, than for your whole body to be cast into hell. Furthermore it has been said, 'Whoever divorces his wife, let him give her a certificate of divorce.' But I say to you that whoever divorces his wife for any reason except sexual immorality causes her to commit adultery; and whoever marries a woman who is divorced commits adultery" (NKJV).

Lust

"The gains of lust is trivial compared with the loss it brings—you forfeit your body eternally for the momentary pleasure of eye or hand. When you have made your eye the instrument of impurity, you cannot see God with it."

Matthew 5: 33–37

"Again you have heard that it was said to those of old, 'You shall not swear falsely, but shall perform your oaths to the Lord.' But I say to you, do not swear at all: neither by heaven, for it is God's throne; nor by the earth, for it is His footstool; nor by Jerusalem, for it is the city of the great King. Nor shall you swear by your head, because you cannot make one hair white or black. But let your 'Yes' be 'Yes,' and your 'No,' 'No.' For whatever is more than these is from the evil one" (NKJV).

telling us that we must deal with sin as drastically and as radically as necessary, and cut off any avenues which we know to be unhelpful to that purity of heart."

CHAPTER 11: TRUTHFULNESS

The position of the church on this passage has varied through the years. The early church interpreted the passage in a manner that prevented "perfect" Christians from swearing at all, while "weaker" Christians were given swearing license within limits. The Reformation Confessions contended that the passage properly interpreted prohibited oaths required by the state in a court of law. A public appeal to God asking him to be a witness constituted an oath. When men use an oath, they invoke God to vouchsafe the truth. Jesus' concern regarding oaths was tied to His concern for complete truthfulness. The very existence of oaths is proof that lies exist. "Jesus destroys the lie by forbidding oaths altogether. . . . The oath must go, since it is a protection for the lie."

When Jesus said, "Let your 'Yes' be 'Yes' and your 'No,' 'No,'" He meant that disciples are accountable for every word they speak, for they are all spoken in His presence. Because Christians are always to speak the truth, oaths are not necessary. In fact, oaths would weaken, not strengthen, a Christian's truthfulness. Thus we are forbidden to swear—period.

When we become disciples, we should realize that complete truthfulness is inseparable from our new life. In fact, because of who Jesus is (John 8:32)—the Truth embodied in living form—the believer, when living in Him, is living in complete truthfulness. This is possible because we have been forgiven and our sin has been removed by Christ. Thus, being untruthful would obviously destroy fellowship, but truth is the basis for all genuine brotherhood.

COMMENTARY

Truthfulness is the sixth element of the extraordinary life of the Christian and is discussed in chapter 12. Truthfulness is presented as a necessary link to Jesus' teaching regarding the swearing of oaths, and Bonhoeffer clearly delivered his understanding of Jesus' burden therein. He stated that Jesus was concerned primarily with complete truthfulness to which oaths often stood as a barrier. Indeed, on occasion, oaths claimed final truth. Herein lay the source of the lie that must be exposed.

CHAPTER 12: REVENGE

As followers of Jesus, Christians give up for His sake "every personal right." After giving up all other things, this is a kind of final test of discipleship. Bonhoeffer believed this passage elaborates on the beatitudes.

"In the Old Testament personal rights are protected by a divinely established system of retribution. . . . to establish a proper community. . . . Jesus takes up this declaration of the divine will and affirms the power of retribution to convict and overcome evil and to ensure the fellowship of the disciples." . . . The right way to requite evil, according to Jesus, is not to resist it. . . . This saying of Christ removes the Church from the sphere of politics. . . . The only way to overcome evil is to let it run itself to a standstill because it does not find the resistance it is looking for. Resistance merely creates further evil and adds fuel to the flames.

Matthew 5: 38–42

You have heard that it was said, 'An eye for an eye and a tooth for a tooth.' But I tell you not to resist an evil person. But whoever slaps you on your right cheek, turn the other to him also. If anyone wants to sue you and take away your tunic, let him have your cloak also. And whoever compels you to go one mile, go with him two. Give to him who asks you, and from him who wants to borrow from you do not turn away" (NKJV).

Violence and exploitation are evil. The only way evil can be overcome is for the disciple to bear witness to it and patiently to endure the evil. Christians can overcome evil by allowing it to play out and patiently enduring it. Bonhoeffer believed that "suffering willingly endured is stronger than evil, it spells death to evil."

COMMENTARY

The seventh ingredient of extraordinary Christian living is identified as nonviolence, outlined in chapter 12. The issue of nonviolence is approached in the midst of a discussion regarding the fact that those called by Jesus renounce their personal rights. Accordingly, Jesus introduced a new way of responding to evil: Let it run its course. Jesus taught that resistance only brought additional evil and in a sense added fuel to the fire.

Hans Kung wrote that Jesus' position is revolutionary: "Love for enemies instead of their destruction, unconditional forgiveness rather than retaliation, readiness to suffer rather that use force, and blessing for peacemakers instead of hymns of hate and revenge." "The most important element in this passage is the strategy that moves from negativism to a positive course of action. The disciple is to be free for God and for his fellow man who needs him. . . . Turning the other cheek is not a surrender but a strategy of operation. This act is to take the initiative in behaving in the freedom of Christ and His love."

CHAPTER 13: THE ENEMY—THE "EXTRAORDINARY"

The whole Sermon on the Mount, believed Bonhoeffer, is summed up in the word *love*. Jesus made clear what He meant by love when He commanded us to love our enemies. We can, thus, have no doubt what He meant. The disciples knew well, according to Bonhoeffer, who the enemy was: i.e., those who accused them of undermining the Jewish faith, of transgressing the Law. The enemies were those who hated the disciples for leaving all for Jesus and who insulted them for weakness and humility. Other enemies saw the disciples as dangerous revolutionaries and wanted them destroyed. Because the disciples refused to be followers of the crowd, they had to endure hostility.

God's will is that we should defeat our enemies by loving them. As Christians we must see our enemy as a brother and, by loving him, repay his hostility. As Christians, our behavior toward our enemies must be determined not by how others treat us but by how Jesus has treated us.

The enemies about whom Jesus was referring are those that are totally unresponsive to the believer's attempts. They are persons who expect everything from the person but also expect to give nothing in return. The command, "love your enemies," requires action. We are not simply to avoid treating them poorly but to proactively engage in heartfelt love for them. The one who follows the call is commanded to "bless those that persecute" and "do good to them that hate you" and "pray for those that despitefully use you and persecute you."

The argument is that love conquers because love for our enemies actually puts us on the path of the cross and into fellowship with Him who suffered there. The more we travel down this road, the more certain is the victory of love over hatred of the enemy. Because then it is not our

Matthew 5:43–48

"You have heard that it was said, 'You shall love your neighbor and hate your enemy.' But I say to you, love your enemies, bless those who curse you, do good to those who hate you, and pray for those who spitefully use you and persecute you, that you may be sons of your Father in heaven; for He makes His sun rise on the evil and on the good, and sends rain on the just and on the unjust. For if you love those who love you, what reward have you? Do not even the tax collectors do the same? And if you greet your brethren only, what do you do more than others? Do not even the tax collectors do so? Therefore you shall be perfect, just as your Father in heaven is perfect" (NKJV).

love which is victorious but Christ's love as expressed on the cross which confronts the enemy. As Christians we realize that we were also once His enemies, and He overcame our hostility with His love. Seen, thus, in the light of the cross, the Christian realizes that his enemy is also an object of the love of God. Both Christian and non-Christian stand beneath Christ's cross, the ultimate symbol of divine love.

 COMMENTARY

The eighth and final element in living the Christian life is identified in this chapter as *love for enemies*. Michael Green identified the key to understanding this element to be the definition of *love*.

> The word "love" is significant. The ancient world knew about philia, friendship; it knew about eros, sexual love; it knew about storage, the love that binds families together; but agape was something very different. That is why the word is practically unknown before Christ . . . For agape means a love which gives itself for the good of the recipient. Of course we cannot like our enemies! But we can love them, in this sense of agape love. We can desire and work for their highest good. We can regard them as those for whom Christ came and died and who are therefore intensely valuable to him. At least, we can begin to move in that direction if we ourselves have been magnetized by the love of God who treats us like that. And it is nothing less than that which Jesus looks for in his disciples.

CHAPTER 14: THE HIDDEN RIGHTEOUSNESS

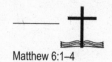

Matthew 6:1–4

Chapter 14 begins with a reminder of chapter 5 where the focus was on the visible nature of the community of the called. There it seemed that a point of distinction for the Christian life was separation from the world. Bonhoeffer stated that this could lead a disciple to adopt an attitude of indifference to the world in which they lived.

Jesus responded to this potential problem in Matthew 6:1–4. Bonhoeffer said that Jesus "calls a halt to the innocent spontaneous joy we get from making our Christianity visible." As Christians we can have the "extraordinary" only when we reflect on how to use these qualities in humility. Even the motive of the disciples for this "better righteousness" must lie beyond us. Again, this righteousness must be visible, but only so that it lights the way to Jesus, and not to us. It is in no way our own righteousness.

This seeming paradox of visibility versus invisibility invites three questions in the journey toward resolution. The questions and his answers are as follows:

1. From whom are we to hide the visibility of our discipleship?

   Not from other men, but from ourselves. When we hide it from ourselves, we can keep our eyes on our Leader and His will. Any righteousness we may possess must be seen in Him. We will then be able to see it not as extraordinary but ordinary and natural. Therefore, in obedience to the teaching of Christ, we must hide the visible from ourselves.

"Take heed that you do not do your charitable deeds before men, to be seen by them. Otherwise you have no reward from your Father in heaven. Therefore, when you do a charitable deed, do not sound a trumpet before you as the hypocrites do in the synagogues and in the streets, that they may have glory from men. Assuredly, I say to you, they have their reward. But when you do a charitable deed, do not let your left hand know what your right hand is doing, that your charitable deed may be in secret; and your Father who sees in secret will Himself reward you openly" (NKJV).

2. How can the visible and the invisible aspects of discipleship be combined, and how can the same life be both visible and hidden?

"To answer this question, all we need to do is to go back to chapter 5 [gospel of Matthew], where the extraordinary and the visible are defined as the cross of Christ beneath which the disciples stand. The cross is at once the necessary, the hidden and the visible—it is the 'extraordinary.'"

3. How is the contradiction between the Matthew 5 and 6 to be resolved?

The meaning of discipleship is the key to understanding the "contradiction" in Matthew. It refers to an "exclusive adherence to" Jesus. We are to follow only Him and look only to Him. But, if the believer looked to the extraordinary quality of the Christian life instead of to Christ, he would no longer be following Jesus.

COMMENTARY

The second part of Section II presents a commentary on Matthew 6 tied together under the title, "Of the Hidden Character of the Christian Life." This part of Section II covers the hiddenness of righteousness, prayer and the devout life, and the simplicity of the carefree life. At first glance this idea of hiddenness seems contradictory to the visible nature of discipleship that Jesus seemed to be teaching just a chapter earlier. In that teaching it seemed that a point of distinction for the community of the called was separation from the world.

As will be seen in the last portion of this section which covers Matthew 7, Jesus calls Christians

How did Bonhoeffer's position of nonviolence impact the role he played in the Confessing Church Movement? What are the differences between judging someone and holding them accountable?

to be separate. What did Jesus mean? How can a disciple be both invisible and seen? Bonhoeffer brings clarity to this issue through several statements made at the end of chapter 14. He said, "All that the follower of Jesus has to do is to make sure that his obedience, following and love are entirely spontaneous and unpremeditated." In doing good we must not let our left hand know what the right is doing. We must be entirely unperceiving of it, or we are simply showing our "own virtue" and not the source of all virtue, Jesus Christ. This is the way the virtue of discipleship can actually live in us—if we are entirely unconscious of the doing of it.

Chapter 14 has as its focus the hiddenness of righteousness. If Christians become aware of their hidden virtue, they are shaping their own reward instead of that which God has planned. When believers become aware of their hiddenness, they move from a posture of dependence to a posture of control. So, ultimately, the issue is not whether righteousness should be hidden or visible but rather what the awareness of righteousness involves. In summary, Bonhoeffer said that certainly righteousness has to be visible. We must be careful "it does not become visible for the sake of becoming visible."

CHAPTER 15: THE HIDDENNESS OF PRAYER

The discussion of this passage regarding prayer begins by pointing out that Jesus taught the disciples to pray. Hence, prayer is a learned not a natural activity. This understanding must be balanced with the reality that "learned" prayer is not the goal, for even prayer that disciplines prayer can be "profitless and void of God's blessing." Prayer for the disciple is a privilege which is allowed only because we are in

Matthew 6:5–13

"And when you pray, you shall not be like the hypocrites. For they love to pray standing in the synagogues and on the corners of the streets, that they may be seen by men. Assuredly, I say to you, they have their reward. But you, when you pray, go into your room, and when you have shut your door, pray to your Father who is in the secret place; and your Father who sees in secret will reward you openly. And when you pray, do not use vain repetitions as the heathen do. For they think that they will be heard for their many words. Therefore do not be like them. For your Father knows the things you have need of before you ask Him. In this manner, therefore, pray: Our Father in heaven, hallowed be Your name. Your kingdom come. Your will be done On earth as it is in heaven. Give us this day our daily bread. And forgive us our debts, As we forgive our debtors. And do not lead us into temptation, But deliver us from the evil one. For Yours is the kingdom and the power and the glory forever. Amen (NKJV).

fellowship with Him. "Only those who, like them, adhere to Jesus have access to the Father through him."

Jesus is the Mediator between God and us. God knows our needs even before we ask. Because of this, as Christians, we can have great confidence and "joyous certainty" in our prayer. The form of the prayer does not matter really. What matters is that our faith lays hold of God and touches the very "heart of the Father who knew us long before we came to him."

Genuine prayer is never just an exercise, pious attitude, or good works. Genuine prayer is really the prayer of a child to God the father. It should never be "given to self-display. . . . Prayer is the supreme instance of the hidden character of the Christian life." It is the opposite of self-exhibition. "When men pray, they have ceased to know themselves, and know only God whom they call upon." Jesus not only taught His disciples how to pray, but He also gave instruction on what to pray. Both the how and the what are exhibited in the Lord's Prayer as contained in these verses of Matthew 6. Here each phrase of the Lord's Prayer is interpreted as follows:

Our Father in heaven,

Disciples are to call upon the heavenly Father as a corporate body. They call upon a Father who already knows his children's needs.

Hallowed be Your name.

God's name of Father, as it has been revealed to the disciples in Jesus Christ, shall be kept holy among them. In His name the whole content of the gospel is embraced.

Your kingdom come.

In Jesus Christ, His followers have witnessed the kingdom of God breaking in on earth. They have seen Satan crushed and the powers of the world, sin, and death broken. The kingdom of God is still exposed to suffering and strife. The little flock has a share in that tribulation.

Your will be done On earth as it is in heaven.

In fellowship with Jesus His followers have surrendered their own wills completely to God's, and so they pray that God's will may be done throughout the world.

Give us this day our daily bread.

As long as the disciples were on earth, they should not be ashamed to pray for their bodily needs. The disciples realized that while it is a fruit of the earth, bread really comes down from above as the gift of God alone. That is why they had to ask for it before they took it. And since it is the bread of God, it is new every day. They did not ask to lay up a store for the future but were satisfied with what God gave them day by day.

Forgive us our debts, As we forgive our debtors.

Every day Christ's followers must acknowledge and bemoan their guilt. Living as they do in fellowship with him, they ought to be sinless, but in practice their life is marred daily with all manner of unbelief. They must pray daily for God's forgiveness.

Do not lead us into temptation,

Many and diverse are the temptations which plague the Christian. Satan attacks him on every side, if haply he might cause him to fall. Sometimes the attack takes the form of a false sense of security, and sometimes ungodly doubt. But the disciple is conscious of his weakness and does

Prayer

What model do you use in your times of personal prayer? Consider using this model as a retreat model for your small group or Sunday school class.

Prayer

"Prayer is the supreme instance of the hidden character of the Christian life. It is the antithesis of self-display. When men pray, they have ceased to know themselves, and know only the God whom they call upon. Prayer does not aim at any direct effect on the word; it is addressed to God alone, and is therefore the perfect example of undemonstrative action."

Matthew 6:16–18

"Moreover, when you fast, do not be like the hypocrites, with a sad countenance. For they disfigure their faces that they may appear to men to be fasting. Assuredly, I say to you, they have their reward. But you, when you fast, anoint your head and wash your face, so that you do not appear to men to be fasting, but to your Father who is in the secret place; and your Father who sees in secret will reward you openly" (NKJV).

Attempting to Imitate Christ's Sufferings

"This is a pious but godless ambition, for beneath it there always lurks the notion that it is possible for us to step into Christ's shoes and suffer as he did and kill the old Adam. We are then presuming to undertake that bitter work of eternal redemption which Christ himself wrought for us. The motive for asceticism was more limited—to equip us for better service and deeper humility."

not expose himself unnecessarily to temptation in order to test the strength of his faith.

But deliver us from the evil one.

The last petition is for deliverance from evil and for the inheritance of the kingdom of heaven. It is a prayer for a holy death and for the deliverance of the church in the day of judgment.

COMMENTARY

The teaching regarding prayer is clear and straightforward. It begins with a discussion that surrounds the nature and purpose of prayer and concludes the chapter by detailing and shedding light on each phrase of the Lord's Prayer. The purpose for the discussion of prayer in the context of these chapters on hiddenness is most accurately expressed in Bonhoeffer's statement that "prayer is the supreme instance of the hidden character of the Christian life."

CHAPTER 16: THE HIDDENNESS OF THE DEVOUT LIFE

Jesus takes it for granted that the disciples will fast. Bonhoeffer believed that, "strict exercise of self-control is an essential feature of the Christian's life." Through such control the Christian is better able to do what God would have them to do. An element of asceticism, Bonhoeffer believed is very important to the Christian. For, if we do not control the desires of the flesh, it will be hard to serve Christ.

Yet discipline alone is not enough to control the desires of the flesh. The only way to deal with the flesh is through faith in Christ. Asceticism is defined as "voluntary suffering" and warns against the danger of being tempted to imitate the sufferings of Christ.

 COMMENTARY

It is clear from this passage that Jesus both upheld the discipline of fasting and anticipated that His disciples would do it. Bonhoeffer reminded the reader that Jesus also warned the disciple about the potential misuse of fasting—again; the issue of hiddenness arises. In his book, *Celebration of Discipline*, Foster stated, "It is sobering to realize that the very first statement Jesus made about fasting dealt with the questions of motive. To use good things to our own end is always the sign of false religion. How easy it is to take something like fasting and try to use it to get God to do what we want."

How focused are you on Christ?

Bonhoeffer defined *simplicity* as a life free from worldly possessions, and he offered the following evaluative questions regarding the simplicity of life:

1. What are you really devoted to?
2. Is your heart set on earthly goods?
3. Do you try to combine devotion to Jesus with devotion to other things?

CHAPTER 17: THE SIMPLICITY OF THE CAREFREE LIFE

Disciples of Jesus must be in communion with Christ. Nothing must be allowed to come between us and the Savior (e.g., the law, personal piety, even the world). As Christians we must always look only to Christ, never Jesus and an admixture of Him and anything else.

Jesus does not prohibit possessing material goods, but they are to be used, not collected. Just as in the wilderness when the Israelites received manna every day, the Christian must rely on God every day. When we store up possessions, we not only spoil the gift but ourselves as well, said Bonhoeffer. When the heart is set on the accumulation of wealth, a clear barrier is put between the believer and God. "Where our treasure is, there is our trust, our security, our consolation and our God." This discussion on possessions informs Jesus' statement, "Do not worry."

COMMENTARY

In chapter 17, two main ideas are presented from Jesus' teaching. The first is captured by Jesus' phrase, "Where your treasure is, there your heart will also be." He asserted that where your treasure is—where your intentions are and your allegiance lies—your heart will be also. Either Christ gets your allegiance, or something or someone else does. Even a small amount of possessions can turn us from Jesus. Where the heart is is the real issue. How do we know where it is? "Everything which hinders us from loving God above all things and acts as a barrier between ourselves and our obedience to Jesus is our treasure, and the place where our heart is."

The second main idea found in this chapter involves the concept of worry. Anxiety makes no sense. Tomorrow, even an hour from now, is beyond our control. Only God holds the key to the future. In regard to worrying about the future, we are "completely powerless." In fact, when we allow ourselves to be taken up in worry, we are in fact "dethroning God" and putting ourselves in His place. The believer must look only to Jesus and His righteousness. We must remember that we are in His hands and under His protection.

"Earthly possessions dazzle our eyes and delude us into thinking that they can provide security and freedom from anxiety. . . . When we seek for security in possessions we are trying to drive our care with care. . . . The way to misuse our possessions is to use them as an insurance against the morrow. . . . The only way to win assurance is by leaving tomorrow entirely in the hands of God and by receiving from him all we need for today."

CHAPTER 18: THE DISCIPLE AND UNBELIEVERS

Matthew 7:1–12

"Judge not, that you be not judged. For with what judgment you judge, you will be judged; and with the measure you use, it will be measured back to you. And why do you look at the speck in your brother's eye, but do not consider the plank in your own eye? Or how can you say to your brother, 'Let me remove the speck from your eye'; and look, a plank is in your own eye? Hypocrite! First remove the plank from your own eye, and then you will see clearly to remove the speck from your brother's eye. Do not give what is holy to the dogs; nor cast your pearls before swine, lest they trample them under their feet, and turn and tear you in pieces. Ask, and it will be given to you; seek, and you will find; knock, and it will be opened to you. For everyone who asks receives, and he who seeks finds, and to him who knocks it will be opened. Or what man is there among you who, if his son asks for bread, will give him a stone? Or if he asks for a fish, will he give him a serpent? If you then, being evil, know how to give good gifts to your children, how much more will your Father who is in heaven give good things to those who ask Him! Therefore, whatever you want men to do to you, do also them, for this is the Law and the Prophets" (NKJV).

Chapter 18 deals with the disciple's potential problem of developing a superior attitude by addressing judgmental attitudes and actions. We must never assume an attitude as disciples to attack others. Rather, we must come to another "with the single-mindedness of the love of Jesus" and an offer of fellowship. It is not our place to judge others. "Judgment is the forbidden objectivization of the other person which destroys single-minded love." We can have our own thoughts about another, but only to the limit that we are afforded an occasion for forgiveness and unconditional love.

In addition to being forbidden to judge, the believer should not force the gospel on others. Attempts to do so are both futile and dangerous. "It is futile, because the swine do not recognize the pearls that are cast before them" (Matt. 7:6). It is dangerous because "we shall only meet the blind rage of hardened and darkened hearts."

COMMENTARY

Section II has included discussions of Matthew 5 which dealt with the extraordinary qualities of the Christian life and Matthew 6 which dealt with the hidden single-hearted righteousness of the disciple. In the final portion of Section II, Matthew 7 is developed to prevent the disciple from believing that he can or should be separated from the rest of society. Chapter 18 directs this prevention through a warning against being judgmental.

The children's story, *Tale of Three Trees*, speaks of the importance of perception and perspective. Each tree had a different perception of what it meant to be important and useful. One tree wanted to be a beautiful treasure chest, and another, a strong sailing ship. The third wanted to stay on the mountainside, growing tall and pointing people to God. Ultimately that perception was changed by a God-given perspective—a perspective of service. What appeared to be a commonplace feeding trough, fishing boat, and scrapwood became a manger, a pulpit, and a cross—tools used by God to change the world forever. This illustrates the first reason we are commanded by Jesus not to judge; things are not always as they appear to be. We can only know in part what God knows in completion. The second principle is that people are ultimately accountable to God, not us. And the third principle is this: As a result of our humanness, we usually judge others to make ourselves feel better. When we are constantly looking for evil in others, we are only trying to justify ourselves and trying to escape punishment for our sins. This is why we pass judgment on others. In fact, we are trying to make God's Word into a double standard, which applies to us in one way and others in a different way.

Judging

"Judging others makes us blind, whereas love is illuminating. By judging others we blind ourselves to our own evil and to the grace which others are just as entitled to as we are. . . . If when we judged others, our real motive was to destroy evil, we should look for evil where it is certain to be found, and that is in our own hearts."

CHAPTER 19: THE GREAT DIVIDE

Matthew 7:13–23

"Enter by the narrow gate; for wide is the gate and broad is the way that leads to destruction, and there are many who go in by it. Because narrow is the gate and difficult is the way which leads to life, and there are few who find it. Beware of false prophets, who come to you in sheep's clothing, but inwardly they are ravenous wolves. You will know them by their fruits. Do men gather grapes from thornbushes or figs from thistles? Even so, every good tree bears good fruit, but a bad tree bears bad fruit. A good tree cannot bear bad fruit, nor can a bad tree bear good fruit. Every tree that does not bear good fruit is cut down and thrown into the fire. Therefore by their fruits you will know them. Not everyone who says to Me, 'Lord, Lord,' shall enter the kingdom of heaven, but he who does the will of

What is meant by the statement that the path of discipleship is narrow and easy to miss?

My Father in heaven. Many will say to Me in that day, 'Lord, Lord, have we not prophesied in Your name, cast out demons in Your name, and done many wonders in Your name?' And then I will declare to them, 'I never knew you; depart from Me, you who practice lawlessness!'" (NKJV).

The Christian church, said Bonhoeffer, "cannot arbitrarily break off all contact with those that refuse his call." All judgment and separation from them must be left to Christ.

The path of discipleship is narrow and easy to miss. It is an easy path from which to stray even after many years of discipleship. The Matthew 7 passage reviewed in this chapter indicates that the separation created by the call of Jesus goes even deeper than previously indicated. It is not just a division between church and world, real Christians and those in name only; but a division "into the very heart of the confessional body." Bonhoeffer reminded us that not everyone who makes the Christian confession will enter the kingdom of heaven. The confessing church itself will be divided.

Even after a confession of faith is made, we are not "saved simply on the ground" that a confession was made. The fact "that we are members of a Church which has a right confession" does not put us in God's favor. Even the church is not marked from the world by "special privilege" but only by God's gracious calling. Bonhoeffer wrote: "Here is the crucial question—has Jesus known us or not?"

COMMENTARY

In chapter 19, Bonhoeffer showed that the separation which the call of Jesus creates goes deeper still. He pointed to the separation that occurs even within the church. "Not everyone that says, Lord, Lord." The point of separation in essence is whether Jesus "knows you." What does being known by Jesus involve? In *Ethics,* Bonhoeffer stated that to be known, one thing is required: "not to hear or do, but to do both in one, in other words to be and to continue in unity with Jesus Christ, to be directed towards him, to receive word and deed."

CHAPTER 20: THE CONCLUSION

Matthew 7: 24-29

"'Therefore whoever hears these sayings of Mine, and does them, I will liken him to a wise man who built his house on the rock: and the rain descended, the floods came, and the winds blew and beat on that house; and it did not fall, for it was founded on the rock. But everyone who hears these sayings of Mine, and does not do them, will be like a foolish man who built his house on the sand: and the rain descended, the floods came, and the winds blew and beat on that house; and it fell. And great was its fall.' And so it was, when Jesus had ended these sayings, that the people were astonished at His teaching, for He taught them as one having authority, and not as the scribes."

Bonhoeffer presented the following concluding remarks for Section II:

"We have listened to the Sermon on the Mount and perhaps have understood it. But who has heard it aright? Jesus gives the answer at the end. He does not allow his hearers to go away and make of his sayings what they will, picking and choosing from them whatever they find helpful, and testing them to see if they work. . . . Humanly speaking, we could understand and interpret the Sermon on the Mount in a thousand different ways. Jesus knows only one possibility: simple surrender and obedience, not interpreting it or applying it, but doing and obeying it. . . . Jesus has spoken: his is the word, ours the obedience."

 **COMMENTARY**

Section II is completed with a concluding chapter that ties together the message of the Sermon on the Mount very simply. Jesus' message is clear, and it invites only one response—obedience.

SECTION-AT-A-GLANCE

CHAPTER 21: THE HARVEST

Chapter 21 opens with Matthew's presentation of Jesus' looking out on the multitudes and being overcome with compassion. Jesus looks with compassion on His people. He was not willing to be satisfied with the small group of disciples who had responded to the call. His disciples had to learn that they would not limit Jesus in His service. His message and His power belonged to the "sick and poor, wherever they were to be found among the people."

Jesus taught that preachers and teachers of the Word must have compassion. People need a shepherd. "Feed my sheep" was the last charge Jesus gave to Peter. The good shepherd:

1. Protects His sheep against the wolf and instead of fleeing, gives His life for the sheep.
2. Knows His sheep by name and loves them.
3. Knows His sheep's distress and weaknesses.
4. Heals the wounded.
5. Gives drink to the thirsty.
6. Sets upright the falling.
7. Leads them gently to pasture.

Matthew 9: 35–38

"Then Jesus went about all the cities and villages, teaching in their synagogues, preaching the gospel of the kingdom, and healing every sickness and every disease among the people. But when He saw the multitudes, He was moved with compassion for them, because they were weary and scattered, like sheep having no shepherd. Then He said to His disciples, 'The harvest truly is plentiful, but the laborers are few. Therefore pray the Lord of the harvest to send out laborers into His harvest'" (NKJV).

"No man dare presume to come forward and offer himself on his own initiative, not even the disciples themselves. Their duty is to pray the Lord of the harvest to send forth labourers at the right moment, for the time is ripe."

8. Leads them the right way.

9. Seeks the one lost sheep and brings it back to the fold.

From a human perspective everything looks hopeless, but Jesus sees things differently. Jesus sees a "field that is ripe unto harvest." It is a great harvest seen only by Christ in His mercy. Jesus is looking for help to carry out the work of harvesting. He cannot do it alone. Who will be the labourers? Only God knows.

 COMMENTARY

The last verses of Matthew 9 presented in chapter 21 form a framework for Section III which focuses on the messengers Christ chooses to use in fulfilling His plan. In the six chapters of this section, the need for workers, the plan for identifying them, and the nature of their leadership are discussed. In addition, the setting and constitution of their work is presented as well as the fruit of the messenger's work.

The Pastor as Shepherd

Can you identify a pastor who has provided this shepherding role in your life? Take a few minutes to write a note of thanks and encouragement to that person.

Chapter 21 points out that Jesus presents a clear message to His disciples: the harvest is great, the laborers are few. In Matthew 9:37, He has articulated the need; and in the final verse (9:38), He presented the plan for having this need met—prayer. Bonhoeffer pointed out that this message is consistent with the Word's presentation of the call—a disciple cannot call himself. Jesus must call him or her, and that call can only be heard and responded to as a result of the power of prayer.

The bulk of this chapter presents a picture of the character required by Jesus' messengers. The picture presented is that of a compassionate shepherd.

CHAPTER 22: THE APOSTLES

God, the Father, revealed His will to the Son. The twelve were called by Jesus and sent into the harvest. Christ anointed them "apostles," messengers, and fellow workers and gave them power to do the work. "So Jesus imparts to them a share in the highest gift he possesses, his power over unclean spirits, and over the devil who has taken possession of the human race." In the Great Commission, Christians become like Christ and are empowered to do Christ's work.

The reader is reminded that there were twelve disciples and this number coincides with a number of other things in Scripture that were recorded in groups of twelve:

1. Twelve tribes of Israel.
2. Twelve thrones that will be prepared for believers in the kingdom.
3. A heavenly Jerusalem with twelve gates on which the names of the twelve tribes are inscribed and twelve foundations bearing the names of the twelve disciples.

The chapter closes with the statement that the only bond of unity among the twelve disciples was Jesus' call and their choice. The call of Jesus surpassed all earlier boundaries and instituted a new and faithful fellowship in Jesus.

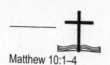

Matthew 10:1–4

"And when He had called His twelve disciples to Him, He gave them power over unclean spirits, to cast them out, and to heal all kinds of sickness and all kinds of disease. Now the names of the twelve apostles are these: first, Simon, who is called Peter, and Andrew his brother; James the son of Zebedee, and John his brother; Philip and Bartholomew; Thomas and Matthew the tax collector; James the son of Alphaeus, and Lebbaeus, whose surname was Thaddaeus; Simon the Canaanite, and Judas Iscariot, who also betrayed Him"(NKJV).

 COMMENTARY

The first messengers Jesus called were the disciples—the apostles. The root of their name makes it clear that the disciples were sent with a purpose. Again, the reader is reminded that

Apostles

There are more than eighty occurrences of the Greek word *apostolos* in the New Testament. It derives from the common verb *apostello*—"to send." This verb frequently is used to communicate the idea of "sending with a purpose." This meaning is consistent with the primary function of the apostles: witness to Christ. This witness was rooted in years of intimate knowledge, experience, and extensive training.

Matthew 10:5–6

"These twelve Jesus sent out and commanded them, saying: 'Do not go into the way of the Gentiles, and do not enter a city of the Samaritans. But go rather to the lost sheep of the house of Israel'" (NKJV).

"Happy are they whose duty is fixed by such a precept, and who are therefore free from the tyranny of their own ideas and calculations."

disciples must not choose to go but rather be sent; they must be commissioned through the call of Jesus. In the next chapter, it is further explained that their work must be defined by Jesus. It must be defined by His purpose, not their own.

The source of the effectiveness of their work is clearly identified—the power given by Jesus. The *Word Biblical Commentary* indicates that not only is the apostle one who is sent with a purpose; he also "shares the authority of the one who sends, as his representative."

CHAPTER 23: THE WORK

Jesus directs the disciples' activity and they are not free to choose their own methods or adopt their own conception of the task. The disciples' work is to be "Christ-work." They are utterly dependent on His will. The disciples must go where they are sent. They don't get to choose a place of work founded on their own preferences or whims.

Additional qualities of the messenger are described. We are reminded that the messenger of Jesus Christ has no personal privileges, title, or fame. In fact, the poverty of the disciple is one of the proofs of his discipleship. These characteristics are an expression of their faith, not in men, but rather in Jesus who called them.

Chapter 26 closes with a discussion regarding the timeliness of the work. The disciples are not to waste time on the mission to which they have been called. "Time is precious, and multitudes are still waiting for the message of the gospel." The disciples should use the greeting that Jesus used: "Peace be to this house."

The discussion of the timeliness of the work includes a message regarding when the disciples are to move on from a house or city. The key to making this decision is the refusal to hear the gospel. Refusing to believe the gospel is "the worst sin imaginable." The disciples "must recognize in fear and amazement both the power and the weakness of the Word of God." When people refuse to hear the gospel, the disciples should not stay in a place "because the Word cannot remain there." They are then commanded to shake the dust from their feet as a sign of the curse which awaits that place.

COMMENTARY

The description of the work of the messenger is consistent with the presentation regarding Jesus' call. Jesus is the one who calls and directs. The disciple's (messenger's) responsibility is to respond with single-minded obedience. Jesus' call and direction for work is driven by His love and is always consistent with His mission. This contrasts with the messenger's *own* zeal and enthusiasm which can easily result in the disciple's straying from Jesus' mission.

"The message becomes an event, and the event confirms the message."

The guidelines for when the messenger should move on to a more receptive audience are clearly presented. These words are offered not only as a decision-making tool but also as a word of encouragement to ministers who are "troubled because their work seems void of success." The lack of response should not be viewed as a sign of ineffectiveness but rather as a sign of lack of receptivity.

Have you ever been in a situation when you felt led to "move on"? What were the factors that shaped your decision?

CHAPTER 24: THE SUFFERING OF THE MESSENGERS

Matthew 10:16–25

"Behold, I send you out as sheep in the midst of wolves. Therefore be wise as serpents and harmless as doves. But beware of men, for they will deliver you up to councils and scourge you in their synagogues. You will be brought before governors and kings for My sake, as a testimony to them and to the Gentiles. But when they deliver you up, do not worry about how or what you should speak. For it will be given to you in that hour what you should speak; for it is not you who speak, but the Spirit of your Father who speaks in you. Now brother will deliver up brother to death, and a father his child; and children will rise up against parents and cause them to be put to death. And you will be hated by all for My name's sake. But he who endures to the end will be saved. When they persecute you in this city, flee to another. For assuredly, I say to you, you will not have gone through the cities of Israel before the Son of Man comes. A disciple is not above his teacher, nor a servant above his master. It is enough for a disciple that he be like his teacher, and a servant like his master. If they have called the master of the house Beelzebub, how much more will they call those of his household!" (NJKV).

Chapter 24 begins with the reminder that there is nothing—failure nor hostility—that can weaken the disciple's certainty that he has been called by Jesus. Again, this call is a source of strength and comfort. They have been sent. Because the disciples did not call themselves, what they are engaged in is "in the strict sense of the word, a *mission*." Thus, Jesus promised them His abiding presence; and, even if they are beset with great danger, nothing can happen to them without His knowledge (see also Matt. 28:16–20).

Though the sending forth warning contained in the Matthew passage carries some sense of uncertainty, it was not intended to do so. For Jesus never called His disciples into a state of supreme certainty. Disciples are called to live by the Word. The disciple must be where the Word is.

If the Word is not heard or accepted, the disciple must yield with it. "But if the Word carries on the battle, the disciple must also stand his ground."

Fear

What are the things that cause fear in your life?

This chapter closes with a brief section on suffering. The disciples will suffer as they answer the call. They will be blamed for divisions and accused of being crazy fanatics. Even in this suffering there is a concealed supernatural power. The disciples will have to stand before the officials of nations "for my sake, for a testimony to them and to the Gentiles." In so doing, their suffering will help their testimony stand.

 COMMENTARY

Clearly presented in the chapter 24 outline of the reality of suffering is the reality of Christ's presence in the midst of that suffering. Suffering is a part of God's plan and Christ's will. This is why the disciples are "given power to make a good confession and deliver a fearless testimony." Christians have the promise of the presence of the Holy Spirit to "make them invincible." When Christians remain true in suffering, God's Word remains true to them.

CHAPTER 25: THE DECISION

Matthew 10:26–39

"Therefore do not fear them. For there is nothing covered that will not be revealed, and hidden that will not be known. Whatever I tell you in the dark, speak in the light; and what you hear in the ear, preach on the housetops. And do not fear those who kill the body but cannot kill the soul. But rather fear Him who is able to destroy both soul and body in hell. Are not two sparrows sold for a copper coin? And not one of them falls to the ground apart from your Father's will. But the very hairs of your head are all numbered. Do not fear therefore; you are of more value than many sparrows. Therefore whoever confesses Me before men, him I will also confess before My Father who is in heaven. But whoever denies Me before men, him I will also deny before My Father who is in heaven. Do not think that I came to bring peace on earth. I did not come to bring peace but a sword. For I have come to 'set a man against his father, a daughter against her mother, and a daughter-in-law against her mother-in-law'; and 'a man's enemies will be those of his own household.' He who loves father or mother more than Me is not worthy of Me. And he who loves son or daughter more than Me is not worthy of Me. And he who does not take his cross and follow after Me is not worthy of Me. He who finds his life will lose it, and he who loses his life for My sake will find it" (NKJV).

We are reminded that our time on this earth is short and that eternity is long. It is decision time. People who have confessed and remained true to God's Word will find Jesus at their side when the judgment hour comes. Jesus will endorse them as His and aid them "when the accuser demands his rights." The whole world will witness Jesus calling the name of the believer before God, the Father. Of course, the reverse is also true. If we were ashamed of Jesus, He will be ashamed of us and deny us in the life to come. The cross is at one and the same time the peace of Jesus and a sword God wielded on earth.

 COMMENTARY

Bonhoeffer was a realist. In this chapter, where he spoke clearly of the necessity of making a decision for Christ, he also addressed one of the major issues that causes many to hesitate to make this decision—fear. Jesus indicated that the decision will result in division—even from family. However, this directive is surrounded by admonition not to fear men. Men may be able to harm the body, but their power ends with death. After death, there is an eternity which they cannot effect. We must overcome the fear of men with fear of God. It is God's judgment that counts. It is the possible eternal destruction of body and soul that counts. "Those who are still afraid of men have no fear of God, and those who have fear of God have ceased to be afraid of men."

What does the text identify as the reward for Christian service?

CHAPTER 26: THE FRUIT

Christians, it is promised, who carry the word of Jesus are His fellow workers and "will be like him in all things." When we are sent out, we must meet others as Christ Himself would meet another. If a disciple is welcomed in, Christ

comes along because we carry His presence. In fact, our job is to bring to the world the most precious gift possible—Christ Himself and the possibility of forgiveness and salvation for eternal bliss, as Augustine said. Here is the reward and fruit for the disciple of their toil and suffering because every service is given to Christ Himself. This means grace for the church and grace for the disciples in equal measure. We must think not of our own suffering or reward but the goal of salvation.

 COMMENTARY

The importance—the fruit—of the messengers and their message is clear. The reception of the message and the messengers amounts to reception of Jesus.

Section IV: The Church of Jesus Christ and the Life of Discipleship

True nature of discipleship

"Discipleship never consists in this or that specific action: it is always a decision, either for or against Jesus Christ."

SECTION-AT-A-GLANCE

CHAPTER 27: PRELIMINARY QUESTIONS

Chapter 27 begins by posing the question, 'How is Jesus' call handed down to us today? In the New Testament, "the call was unmistakable but for us it is a highly problematical and uncontrollable decision." Bonhoeffer then went on to point out that the wrong question is being asked. Contrasting the situation of the apostles and the believer today can be too strongly drawn. The believer must not forget that Jesus is not dead but alive and speaking to us today. Jesus is to be found in the church through the ministry of Word—preaching—and in the sacraments. No personal revelation is needed to hear Jesus's call: Listen to the gospel of the crucified and risen Lord Jesus. This is all that is needed.

Object of Jesus' command

"The object of Jesus' command is always the same—to evoke whole-hearted faith, to make us love God and our neighbour with all our heart and soul."

Christ's call can be taken in many different ways. What we think of Jesus will determine how we respond. He can be recognized only by faith. In this regard, it is for us just as it was for the first Christians. They saw and believed. We hear the Word and believe.

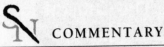

COMMENTARY

Section IV completes Bonhoeffer's *The Call to Discipleship*. He concluded the book with this section that outlines his doctrine of the church. Included in the presentation is a discussion of the close connection between discipleship and churchmanship, the means by which the call is heard in the context of the church and the marks of the church. He placed a strong emphasis on the role of Word and sacrament and returned to themes of the suffering and visibility of the believer that have been explored throughout the text.

Chapter 27 offers an answer to the question, How can Jesus' call be heard today? This question is often asked as a means of escaping the call. The person posing the question offers it with the filter: "How can I hear the call of Jesus? It was easy for the disciples. They were there with Jesus in the flesh. But what about me?" The questioner is challenged to look for the call where it can be received. For the disciples it was in the physical presence of Jesus; for the believer today, it is in the Word and sacraments. Jesus is not dead, rather He is alive and is the only one to whom we must listen for the call. "Hear the Word, receive the Sacrament; in it hear him himself, and you will hear his call."

CHAPTER 28: BAPTISM

"Baptism is essentially passive—being baptized, suffering the call of Christ. In baptism man becomes Christ's own possession. . . . From that moment he belongs to Jesus Christ. He is wrested from the dominion of the world, and passes into the ownership of Christ." Baptism represents the breaking in by Christ into the realm of Satan. This breaking in and claiming was established through the life, death and Resurrection of Jesus and is effected in the believer's life through baptism.

Baptism represents the believer's becoming Christ's possession, resulting in the believer's submission to the cross which brings suffering. "The cross to which we are called is a daily dying in the power of the death which Christ died once and for all. In this way baptism means sharing in the cross of Christ."

Even though baptism is "a passive event" for the person being baptized, it is never a mechanical process. The Holy Spirit is the gift of baptism, Christ Himself living in the hearts of the believer. When we are baptized, we become the house where the Holy Spirit dwells. The Holy Spirit is the pledge of the abiding presence of and fellowship with Jesus.

Jesus' call required a visible act of obedience. Following Jesus was and is a public act. Likewise, baptism is a public event which means "a member is grafted on to the visible body of Christ."

COMMENTARY

Bonhoeffer contended that in baptism Jesus claims His own and designs the church. Baptism represents the believer's becoming Christ's possession. It is a rite of entry to the body of Christ and offers the fruit of the Holy Spirit.

In the closing paragraphs of this chapter, the importance of the visible nature of baptism is discussed. This discussion parallels a central

The Call

"The only constant factor throughout is the sameness of Christ and of his call then and now. His word is one and the same, whether it is addressed during his earthly life to the paralyzed or the disciples, or whether it is speaking to us today."

Romans 6:3

"Or do you not know that as many of us as were baptized into Christ Jesus were baptized into His death?" (NKJV).

Baptism

"Baptism therefore betokens a breach. Christ invades the realm of Satan, lays hands on his own, and creates for himself his Church."

73

theme found throughout the text—the visible nature of discipleship. The life of the disciple is not to be hidden, and baptism in a sense inaugurates that visibility through the public ritual and celebration.

CHAPTER 29: THE BODY OF CHRIST

Chapter 29 begins by asking how we today can have a similar communion and fellowship with Jesus as that experienced by the disciples who enjoyed the bodily presence of Jesus. Paul indicated that we are members of the body of Christ through baptism. "It is certain that there can be no fellowship or communion with him except through his body. For only through the Body can we find acceptance and salvation." So how do we participate in this body? Answer: through two sacraments, baptism and the Lord's Supper. Preaching is not enough to engraft us in Christ's Body. Baptism includes us in the unity Christ's body. The Lord's Supper nurtures and supports our fellowship and communion in the body. "The communion of the body of Christ, . . . is the sign and pledge that we are 'with Christ' and 'in Christ,' and that he is 'in us.'"

The body of Christ is the church. After His ascension, the church has become the body of Christ. Christ is really present in the church. "We should think of the Church not as an institution but as a person, though of course a person in a unique sense."

This chapter concludes with insights into Scripture's definition of *the body*. First, the head of the body is Jesus which reminds the believer of the importance of the lordship of Christ. Jesus is the one who oversees, directs, and coordinates the activity of the body. Also, the body is made up of many parts. Because the church is made up of many members, no one can transcend its own individuality. For example, the hand can't take the place of the eye, etc. Each maintains separate identity and function. On the other hand, their identity is only maintained as members of a fellowship united in service. The unity of the church makes each part what he is, the fellowship what it is. Christ and His body make the church what it is.

How is the Body of Christ made visible in the world?

COMMENTARY

The teaching in this book regarding the body of Christ is clear. It is through Christ, the head of the body, that we find acceptance and salvation. We participate in the body through the sacraments of baptism and the Lord's Supper. And the body of Christ is the church.

The Body of Christ

"The Body of Christ is the place of acceptance, the place of atonement and peace between God and man. God finds man in the Body of Christ, and man finds himself accepted by God in that same body."

Of particular interest is the discussion of the description of the body of Christ as a collective person rather than an institution. Here we have an accurate highlight of the important reality of the body. The body, the church, is organic, an organism that functions not according to an organizational chart but rather through the intricate networks of relationships that can only be paralleled by the understanding of the complexity of the human body.

CHAPTER 30: THE VISIBLE COMMUNITY

As a consequence of the Incarnation, the church, the body of Christ, is visible. "A truth, a doctrine, or a religion need no space for themselves. . . . They are heard, learnt and apprehended, and that is all." But Jesus needs the ears and hearts of living men to follow Him. So He calls Christians to a literal, bodily following. The living Word both called them and created their

Sacraments

In everyday usage the word *sacrament* had been applied in two ways: (1) as a pledge or security deposited in public keeping by the parties in a lawsuit and forfeited to a sacred purpose; (2) as the oath taken by a Roman soldier to the emperor, and thence to any oath. These ideas later combined to produce the concept of a sacred rite which was a pledge or token, the receipt of which involved an oath of loyalty, and this led in time to the limitation of the word *sacrament* to the two major rites of divine institution: Baptism and the Lord's Supper.

bodily fellowship with Him. Thus, "they could no longer remain in obscurity, for they were the light that must shine."

The manner in which the body is made visible is elaborated. First, the church is made visible through the preaching of the Word.

The teaching of the apostles and prophets, which was a witness of Christ's revealing Himself, is the foundation on which the church is built. The cornerstone of the church is Jesus Christ Himself.

The church is made visible secondly through the expression of spiritual gifts. "When this Word comes, the Holy Spirit comes, showing to Christians, both individually and corporately, the gifts of the incarnate Christ." The third and fourth expressions of visibility are identified as Baptism and Communion. "In the two sacraments he encounters us bodily and makes us partakers in the fellowship; and communion of his Body. . . . The Body of Christ becomes visible to the world in the congregation gathered round the Word and Sacraments."

The fifth and final element of visibility is identified as the work of ministry. The church, the body, is made visible through the ministries in which it serves. The ministries of the church are not to be limited to traditional outreach ministries. Every act a Christian does is in reality "part of the common life of the Church of which he is a member. . . . Wherever we are, whatever we do, everything happens 'in the body,' in the Church, 'in Christ.'"

COMMENTARY

In essence, this chapter provides a synthesis of thoughts on the nature of life as a disciple and as a member of the body of Christ, the church. The two are inextricably connected. The theme of the visibility of the believer is amplified in chapter 30's discussion of the visible community. In the life of the disciple, the body of Christ is made visible in the following five ways:

1. Preaching of the Word
2. Expression of spiritual gifts
3. Rite of Baptism
4. Celebration of the Lord's Supper
5. Work of Ministry

The body of Christ claims space and therefore claims "living-space." The body, the disciple, must stay in the world.

CHAPTER 31: THE SAINTS

Christ's church, the *ecclesia Christi*, is a community of disciples and, as such, no longer belongs to the world. Of course, it still lives in the world; but it is no longer of this world. As the holy church, the community of the saints, its members are saints, "sanctified in Jesus Christ, chosen and set apart before the foundation of the world. The object of their calling in Jesus Christ, and of their election before the foundation of the world, was that they should be holy and without blemish."

God's primary purpose is expressed as being the establishment of a holy community, a community of saints, and further asserts that this is accomplished in the body of Christ. As such, the church is "the peculiar possession of God" and

Staying in the World

"To stay in the world with God means simply to live in the rough and tumble of the world and at the same time remain in the Body of Christ, the visible Church, to take part in its worship and to live the life of discipleship. In so doing we bear testimony to the defeat of this world."

Ephesians 1:4

"Just as He chose us in Him before the foundation of the world, that we should be holy and without blame before Him in love" (NKJV).

is a sanctuary in the world and separated from sin. This has been accomplished by God Himself becoming man, taking upon Him our flesh in Jesus and in His body bearing our flesh to the death of the cross. This righteousness is given to the believer. Desiring an "independent righteousness of our own" forfeits our only chance of justification which comes only through the righteousness of God.

The bulk of the remainder of chapter 31 is spent discussing the differences between justification and sanctification. "Justification is the means whereby we appropriate the saving act of God in the past, and sanctification the promise of God's activity in the present and future." With justification we found entrance into fellowship and communion with Christ through the unique and final event of His death. Sanctification keeps us in Christ's fellowship and means that Christians have been judged already and are being preserved until the coming of Christ.

This has threefold significance for the church: First, sanctification is maintained by being clearly separated from the world. Second, sanctification is maintained by walking worthy of God's holiness. And, third, sanctification is hidden as we wait for the day of Jesus Christ.

 COMMENTARY

Christ's messengers are called saints, those that are sanctified in Jesus Christ. In fact, the very object of the calling of the disciples was and is the establishment of the process of sanctification, the process of being made pure and "without blemish." This process is intended to occur in the context of community— the body of Christ.

CHAPTER 32: THE IMAGE OF CHRIST

The promise here surpasses understanding; but when we follow Christ, we are destined to bear His image. Yet the ideal of conforming to the image of Christ is not to be striven after. It is the "form of Christ which seeks to be formed in us." We cannot transform ourselves into His image. It is Christ's work in us which is not finished until He has perfected us. "We must be assimilated to the form of Christ in its entirety, the form of Christ incarnate, crucified and glorified."

In this short concluding chapter, we are offered an understanding of what is involved in the disciple's process of being conformed to Christ's image. The process of conformation is not so much an imitation of Christ as it is the welcoming of the development of Christ's image in the life of the believer. When a person accepts Christ, he or she is "in Christ," "with Christ," and "Christ is in him or her." So the process of becoming like Christ is the process of "getting out of the way," the process of allowing Christ to be revealed in the believer's life.

Sanctification

Sanctification has its roots in the Latin word *sanctus*, which means holy. It is a term traditionally used to describe the process in which:

1. The Holy Spirit continually gives new life to the believer.
2. The believer is released from the power of sin and guilt.
3. The believer is enabled to love God and to serve his neighbor.

Romans 8:29

"For whom He foreknew, He also predestined to be conformed to the image of His Son, that He might be the firstborn among many brethren" (NKJV).

BIBLIOGRAPHY

Augsburger, Myron S. *The Communicator's Commentary*. Matthew. Ed., Lloyd J. Ogilvie, ed. Dallas: Word Publishing, 1982.

Bethge, Eberhard. *Dietrich Bonhoeffer*. Ed., Edwin Robertson. Trans., Eric Mosbacher, Peter and Betty Ross, Frank Clarke and William Glen-Doepel, New York: Harper and Row, 1970.

Bonhoeffer, Dietrich. *Cost of Discipleship*, New York: Macmillan Publishing Co., Inc., 1949.

Bonhoeffer, Dietrich, *Ethics*. New York: Collier Books, Macmillan Publishing Company, 1955.

Bonhoeffer, Dietrich. *Life Together*. Trans., John W. Doberstein. New York: Harper & Bros., 1954.

Bonhoeffer, Dietrich. *The Way to Freedom: Letters, Lectures and Notes: 1935–1939*. Ed., Edwin Robertson. Trans., Edwin Robertson and John Bowden. New York: Harper & Row, 1966.

Douglas, J. D. *New Bible Dictionary*. Wheaton: Tyndale House Publishers, 1962.

Fant, Clyde E. and Pinson, William M. *Treasury of Great Preaching*. Dallas: Word Publishing, Inc., 1995.

Foster, Richard. *Celebration of Discipline*. San Francisco: Harper and Row, 1978.

Green, Michael. *Matthew for Today*. Dallas: Word Publishing, 1988.

Guelich, Robert. *A Foundation for the Understanding of the Sermon on the Mount*. Dallas: Word Publishing, 1982.

Hagner, Donald A. *Word Biblical Commentary 33A*. Ed., David A. Hubbard, Glenn W. Barker, John D. W. Watts, and Ralph Martin. Dallas: Word Publishing, Inc. 1993.

Harvey, Van A. *A Handbook of Theological Terms*. New York: Macmillan Publishing Company, 1964.

Kelly, Geffrey B.. *Liberating Faith: Bonhoeffer's Message for Today*. Minneapolis: Augsburg Publishing House, 1984.

Kung, Hans. *On Being Christian*. New York: Doubleday, 1976.

Lucado, Max. *The Applause of Heaven*. Dallas: Word Publishing, 1990.

Marsh, Charles. *Rediscovering Dietrich Bonhoeffer*. New York: Oxford University Press, 1994.

Microsoft® Encarta® 96 Encyclopedia Funk and Wagnalls Corporation.

Placher, William C., *A History of Christian Theology*. Philadelphia: The Westminster Press, 1983.

Union Seminary Quarterly Review. vol. 1, no.3, March 1946.

Wesley, John. *A Plain Account of Christian Perfection*. London: Epworth Press, 1952.

SHEPHERD'S NOTES

SHEPHERD'S NOTES

SHEPHERD'S NOTES

SHEPHERD'S NOTES